2 ◄ RVP100

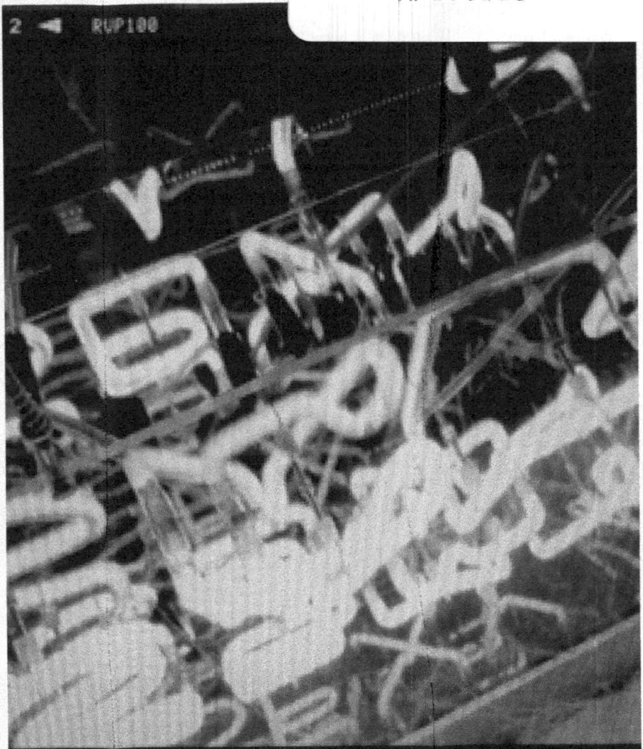

MIND-PUSH: VERSE OF DAY/NIGHT

MIND-PUSH VERSE

PHILLIP BALDWIN

for Nathalie

ALL S IS

SOME S

P

IS P

NO :

SOM

P

IS N

rough road

phillip baldwin

MIND-PUSH: VERSE OF DAY-NIGHT

These are a series of 'generative' verses on the themes of willing oneself through urban landscapes. They are (supposedly the first such thing!) to be read and or performed aloud in an infrared point cloud so that the body's movement through a quadrant will playback what was said seconds or minutes before thus distorting time, simulation, and archive. This distortion of time through past and present is further sectioned into Aristotelian quadrants that negate, obverse, or contradict what was perform before. Another interface that these verse poems are meant to interact with is the neuro-sensor that can distort time to 'future' recordings or past declamations of the verse.

All of these gimmicks and prosthesis alternate between the simplicity of just 'listening' to the performance (or reading on 'obsolete' paper!) or becoming aware of the intended or unintended formal complexity of human and machine performing with the intended or unintended chance and effect. What is the writer's intention? What is the performer's intention? What is the listener's intention? As much of pre-modernist and modernist expression assumed set categories and lexicons of original reproduction, representation, and legitimacy this non-experiment in text and performance, archive and simulation, begins with a premise that information now travels at the speed of light and now has the tendency to remove notions of 'the past' and 'the future'. Where do we find legitimacy behind the multiple tiny screens that we encounter every day? How

ALL S IS P

NO S IS P

SOME S IS P

SOME S IS NOT P

can we expand our critical authority and a sense of 'will' out of the imploded present? This book of verse on dwelling in the surging urban night and day attempts to express some of these questions in this McLuhanesque 'mashup'.

rough road
phillip baldwin

Rough road

Night highway wager:
travel through humid
Roads with nothing but
truckers and drunks.
The speed with which
they push you
Over construction crew
gauntlets
(Do they hold their
coffee and donuts
there too in the dark)
Six guys watching two
At the grinder.
This

Yes this…
Over bashed
roads of day
Roman
ambition to
network the
empire…
Makes you
Wonder
what
Night of
nothing is
best to die in
Gnarled
metal?

ALL S IS
SOME S
P
IS P

Back at four

NO S
SOME
P
IS NC

Coffee
Thousands of bumps
You wonder which
Demon technology
Put together your car
Or why it still runs.

Late night
romance of
continuing
As if it will
always stay dark
As if this were
the best place to
be
In your life

rough road
phillip baldwin

Like you did
In a hot summer attic of
Granddad's national Geographic's
That went back before world war one.
This was a one of the few times
(Even before 'smartphones')
That I knew I was at
Where I should be.

There could be a war out there
And nobody would know
In/outside of the one of the busiest
Cities on earth
East coast
Moves in potholes
Each as flak in
Your
Bomber movie.

Ugly mothers
breed that night
And …as you
park
In a place you
can't believe
You have
Hot
Insects
Humid
And a waterfall
On the back of
your neck
You hear a
white man
scream
From a
basement
apartment:

ALL S IS
SOME S
P
IS P

NO S IS
SOME S
P
IS NOT P

'I can't believe your
attitude about the worse
thing that has ever
happened to me!'

Yes. No Schadenfruede
from you.
Take it on the chin buddy
From your comfortable rent
or own…
She wants out.
And you
In this deep night are
lucky…
Move on

ugh road
llip baldwin

She likes that you still care
Late at night to break the silence.
Drama queen.
Suburban now urban chicks
Talk of the syllogisms
Of job ambition, love, and child.
Missing the law of the excluded middle:
You.

You are lucky and don't know it on
The edge of four in the humid morning
Heavy rain still glazes the street.
A pink slip is a bullet dodged...
Join me and the rabid truckers
Pushing steel
On half-way gigs

Productive
Optimistic in the
infinite night
Ugly girls will still
be the ones to
poop out the
babies
You will have the
illusion/and the
real
Of making good o
the productive
night.
Make it...move
Terrorize the cars
With demon rigs
And sleep like
suckling pigs
As Jersey food
stops
In your cab
AC or not.

ALL S IS
SOME S
P
IS P

N
S
P
IS

It is better that your present
That you can't believe
As I cant believe
I made it back in a piece
After a potlatch gig

Spending vanity of
utopian ideas
On the façade of
Independence Hall.
Scream to the night.
And then be
released.

rough road

phillip baldwin

The logic of near awakened dream

Is it this time I think of
Each hour of yesterday?
The woods…the colony.
The shore harbor…the deep green.
Is this
The time
That
On the stage of the hippocampus
I place
A humid sunny stroll

down
Through the
brownstones?
It is the best
time to
restage
To re
Work.
Is this the
time I forget?
What it is

ALL S IS

SOME S
P

IS P

NO S IS

SOME S
P

IS NOT P

To forget in sleep
Roads and residencies…
Times where it is only
Myself
Who is the future reader…the friend
Perhaps
In the future.

Friends and
lovers
disappoint.
That is their
job.
As I, probably,
have
disappointed
Others
In my
Wanting.

hore and woods of the dream

illip baldwin

Who is the horseman to
The horse of my waking?
Who will tell me what to awaken
to?
What sort of list is not banal?
What sort of day does not call me
out?
Cloudless

Hot like democracy
Where the weak
wait...
Where I can figure
who
Doesn't like
working at all
Or who hasn't
worked in two
generations.
I work hard on my
eight

ALL S IS

SOME S

P

IS P

NO

SOM

P

IS N

And then in my four or five free
I try to escape like the birdman
Seen in exhibition
Fragments of a self
Then come together as another animal
Fragments in a

dream of sleep then
Awakened.
We 'freelance' in
dreams
And make our little
hunting and gathering.
We 'work' at jobs
And make sex and

shore and woods of the dream

phillip baldwin

sleep a job also.
What should be fun?
What has become fun?
Is interpreting
The liminal spaces
Between
What was formerly fun...
Making out,
Spewing liquid words
After sleep
Between dreams and waking
Where every illogical thought is

An insect
For insects
specialize
I am a human
waking.
The walk in the
heat
Is liminal also
Of and between
stasis and
departure
What a game I
could make of
the 'Tempest'
Spilled out

ALL S IS
SOME S
P
IS P

NO S IS
SOME S
P
IS NOT P

Figures going feral as if in a dream
To rebel against
Colonial order.
What an illusion that order was...
To land in wilderness
And to start chopping trees as if

in a dream
And starve
wholesale
What figures in
the dream?
The aboriginals
were
Are
They watch from

shore and woods of the dream

hillip baldwin

the woods
And then
As they could kill the
pathetic/starved
Whites
They
Say
Mostly to the women
And kids
Enter the woods and
leave
The half-baked idea of
Colony
Of the 'civilized'
Of one god
Of a demi-god who
suffered
For your sin of
colonizing.

Even the
conscious da
He hangs as pro
That you will be
illogicall
Spiked in the side
For your first tes
of defying the
fathe
Leaving 'mother
country'
And you will die
like women in
Starvation.
Or drink to call up
dreams on the
edge
Of the forest

ALL S IS

SOME S

P

IS P

NO

SO

P

IS

What kind of strange man is this?
Who hangs on a cross?
Thought the red men.
And for this they steal the land that is
Already theirs?
They kill in the name

Of the civilized.
This hanging man
makes them illiterate
To the entire speaking
world
Around: the edge of
the shore
The deep of the

shore and woods of the dream

phillip baldwin

green.
What
kind of
strang
e
'father
' is
only
above
?
Imagin
ed and
consta
ntly
makes
Sadisti
c tests
to
prove
obedie
nce?

This never
helps you
listen
To blank
Tabula rasa
That you are
here
Where
You might die
And with that
They
'vanished' into
the liminal
woods

ALL S IS

SOME S
P

IS P

NO S IS

SOME S
P

IS NOT P

Between colony of reason
And
Land of every living deity
Who could give
And take.
What those don't and who don't
Think
That this feral move is yours

Every night.
The oral bottle is the big tit
The perspective grid...
To half slumber
But to those
Perspectival,
Lost,
Movement into woods of
sleep
Is merely best relief.

...ore and woods of the dream

...llip baldwin

MIND-PUSH VERSE

PHILLIP BALDWIN

PACKAGING AIR AND DREAMS

Use is shaped by format: what is the
real use of sleep?
Perhaps we can look at the stopping...
the hard wall of
The alarm clock
The bulk of
The weekend spent trying to
Stay
Listening to dreams
The last dreams of the morning
Most fertile
Because they have/are the most
Remembered
I can barely think of the house in this
last one
How children are grown on credit now
How

All a very surprised that
they but on
The middle class
garments
With big middle class
debt.
Children, life,
continued,
Is the ultimate
commodity
Potlatch
Giving it to all
Accomplished
Visceral
And then there is
education
Knowledge
Knowing
They put a price on that
From the start.
There was a time when
children where public
They belonged to all of
the community
To watch

S IS P

NO S IS P

E S IS P

And they did
And there was a time
When knowledge
Was that?
Found with
The love of dusty
Dank
Mildewed libraries
As that smell turned a whole
generation on

SOME S IS NOT P

The road maps of living
better
Different.
There will come a time
when air and dreams
Will also be
commodities?
The last
To turn from

Public bounty
But how will they turn either
Into that simple thing
They can sell back to you?
They could start.... like water....
To make it dirty
And then to make it packaged in
beautiful
Slender bottles
Like a fetish of a mother's love
Then
They could say
This designed container
Holds the last of the clean air
The clean, public, dreams
Buy what is inside and get this
Beautiful container for free.
Inside and out.
With air and dreams we could
Grumble and bitch

Like petulant
consumers
That this isn't what we
thought
Would be the latent
from the manifest
But what would purge
this world
Even, as the evil have
planned,
To make us think the
world is one big thing
That we deserve as
commodities?
The knowledge,
The children,
The house,
The food,
The
Air?

ALL S IS P

NO S IS P

SOME S IS P

SOME S IS NO

Could we
Bring those
Rogue back
With guilt?
Like the cop
Who started shooting
The families of
Corrupt cops
And,

From his social media
Gives advices on
Everything he sees
Like a pulpit
Before going
underground
To scare more corrupt
cops?
They way they seal
up the dream
Is interpreting
Them as a pipeline,
A stream

RE-PACKAGING AIR AND DREAMS
phillip baldwin

That contains the latent
Authority
That you have to buy
Guilty of the death of dad
You are willing to buy back
Air
And then dreams
As the rest of the free
Is sold by
Those lucky to stand on the spigot
Of false authority.

S IS P

NO S IS P

ME S IS P

SOME S IS NOT P

RE-PACKAGING AIR AND DREAMS

phillip baldwin

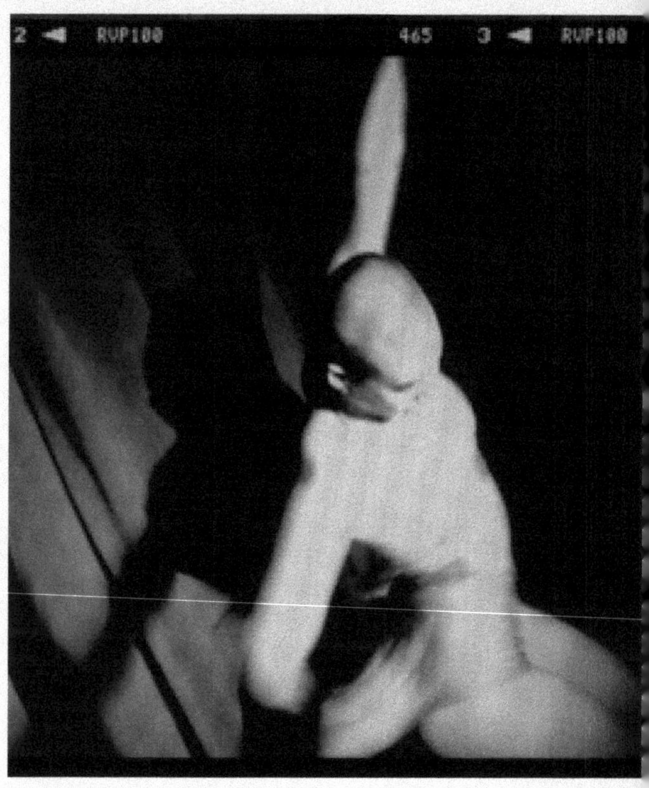

MIND-PUSH VERSE

PHILLIP BALDWIN

APERSPECTIVAL

Pair bond, pack bond:
Leave mammalian
Anomie, alienation, anxiety
Behind or between.
Egg slicer
Orthoganals
Cut
And cut
The space of
Your despair
Into smaller units of
Despair.

When the white man
In the first blush
Of neuro-economics
Toward paper money
Saw African masks
He/she was secretly
Entranced.
Here was another way
out!
The failure of the
mammal
Pack bond
With imperial boats
Was replaced
With a heaven and
hell
Found i

And the thin air
Welfare society
Was in its first

ALL S IS

SOME S
P

IS P

NO S IS

SOME S
P

IS NOT P

n money…
Now they needed
Thos calculations of infinite
Egg slicers
Over the space of
'Yet to be conquered people'
At the very time their
Pack bond
Stayed thin

meager blush.
On the shores
of
People they
herded into
camps
Enslaved by
other blacks
Taking them
from the
Right side

(to Gebser this is where
Innovation comes)
Right to left
To the left coast
Bound for Brazil
Caribbean
And America
There they saw
Masks…

Overjoyed
In secret
Where they:
Another view.
Another
Push out of
The consciousness
Of
The one point view
Which is the same as

Held by the 'new le
One vie
Here there are ma
mas
Theory of mas
Theory of
Not magic
As accounted
Out of pair and pack
But an explosion of
time
Out of space.
Here the African
mask
Mapped the time
An individual
Could play
Clay like
With

ALL S IS

SOME S
P

IS P

N
S
P
IS

Dasein
Or
Little times
Within big.
Poverty
Is real
Paper lack
Is the lack of pack.
They
The slavers
Did bring back
The masks
And

Here the
painters-
cartographers
Of nothing-
Said that we
were missing
time…
Plastic time
Time without
pack-money
Pair bonding
Anxiety

aperspectival
phillip baldwin

Picasso wasn't afraid
To look at the masks
Nor take another woman
As inspiration.
Of grubbing
Real shame for lacking
Mammalian pacts
Like hunters
Killers

Who could meet the slavers
And say
We will sell your painters
Masks instead.

No trick
But this
Is what you came for
anyway?
Means to mask your
poverty
For you have bonded
Only to chase paper
As you could never
Pick up a hitchhiker
Or trust a neighbor
Like the one who
killed his
Teacher-wife
And stuffed her in

ALL S IS

SOME S
P
IS P

the
Basement wall
In a bag
And photographed
Women from his house
With a tele-photo.
We give you back a mask

NO S IS

SOME S
P
IS NOT P

That isn't the
infinite space
Of anxiety
Of lack
Lack of pack
Faustian
Faux
Form
For
Here is mask....

perspectival
phillip baldwin

Here
enters
time
As the
fourth
dimen
sion
As you
will try
With
your
libertar
ian
mistak
es
To

Egg slice
Reasons why
You must
enslave
We sell you
masks
Or better
Give them
(As they did
rhythm to jazz)
And give these
to your seers
Of another
Space

ALL S IS

SOME S
P

IS P

NO

SO
P

IS

Of pack bonding
Pair bonding in pleasure
Not pride of patriarch
And give
These
To your children
To see

Feel
That infinity
Does not come
as a bargain
With poverty
devils
It comes
As a gift
With time.

aperspectival
phillip baldwin

MIND-PUSH VERSE

PHILLIP BALDWIN

ENHANCES

P ZOMBIES

Things that look alive like
designer water
Training
Obedience
Take it all at face value.

Accept the fall over the cliff.

REVERSES INTO

Reverses into
The first challenge
Of the castrating father.
Accept his
Territory
The alpha
To lean
That he has one woman
Your mother.
Then, as with stealth
The challenge the second
time
Reverses into
Acceptance
If
You succeed.

ALL S IS

SOME S

P

IS P

NO S

SOME

P

IS NO

RETRIEVES

You retrieve
All that was
All that was
Building skyscrapers
Individual infinity.
Older ground
Humid smelling
Night forests
Always
The truth
Emerges in
The scent

OBSOLESCES

Of the thing
The way they spray
The way that they set their
territory.
Not amplified
Here is the territory
Castrate not the invisible
alpha....
Moving around
Castrate not...the medium
Of the cloud
Moving above

approach something from the cliche

PHILLIP. BALDWIN@gmail.com

ENHANCES

Now they learn more
From there-the cloud...
Then pathetic sprayings of
invisible ground.

REVERSES INTO

They crave brain or blood
as if
The spied on Americans
wish
Their narcissistic dreams
To spill forth
In vortices
Of importance.

S IS

E S

NO S IS

SOME S

P

IS NOT P

RETRIEVES

Most don't live lives before
Necessary to be spied
upon.
Grandiosity
Obsolescent infinity
Of the individual life.

OBSOLESCES

Obsolesces
Zombies or humans
Big movies
Pervasive TV
Always about things
That seem to
Stand upright
Like human apes
Move slowly or fast
Doesn't matter. Rabid
Or lethargic

proach something from the cliche

P. BALDWIN@gmail.com

ENHANCES

Sex, death, and narcissism
In-between.
Reflection of the self
In the other
The cloud of others.
Cast big
Moving

REVERSES INTO

Memes with age.... spread
You are the zombie stuffed with
The marrow of money not memes.
You are the minion:
With minions...
Like the hoards that climb over
Fences/walls
To take back the living
To bring them to the undead.

ALL S IS

SOME S

P

IS P

NO

SO

P

IS N

RETRIEVES

But these undead
Have no narcissism
Unlike you.
So spray.
And know that one-day
The father will be
Brought down.
You will gather the females
Or the one. You will take...

OBSOLESCES

Apart
Span.
And to naturalize the killing
Of zombies
Is like turning food
Into a luxury
Next, the air.

approach something from the cliche

PHILLIP. BALDWIN@gmail.com

MIND-PUSH VERSE

PHILLIP BALDWIN

Mammals and art

That gender is the most
deadly
Direct
Through indirection….
Setting and waving
Traps
That no faint of heart
misogynist
Can see
Always suspect like a
paranoid.

Hardly sweet like their
daddy's
Put them on the pedestal
If they had a daddy.
Every pussy hound thinks
they know
The ropes
Nope.

Glide in
the hot
night
Wearing
Just
Loose
fitting
dresses
With bare
shoulders
Cities have
them thick.
Cities have
them by
the dump
truck.

ALL S IS

SOME S
P

IS P

NO S

SOM
P

IS N

Places where old fat pedagogues
And
Suburban
Benchwarmers can't go…

Youth and
beauty is
something to
envy
For a little bit.
Man-syllogisms
don't fit
One mood
Cut losses
The female
Makes thick
Tar
Pits

mammals and art

phillip baldwin

Beneath all
Attraction
Makes
Time to deposit eggs
Think
Of dropping eggs

Everywhere
Including
The laps of beta females/when they get old
They turn to pedagogy

Like a
Weapon
Or reason
Or the rules
They expect
You to know always.

Then the perfume
whiff
Smell…smell it scant
On the pretty ones
who
Dart and duck
And dive
Around
Rules of the game.
Make you pay

Or
Spend before you
pay
And make you
Think
Why do you enjoy
their company?
Without quid pro quo

ALL S IS
SOME S
P
IS P

NO S IS
SOME S
P
IS NOT P

How do you set the quid pro quo?
Obligation.
The way they made your pride
And chivalry

Ants in the
ape-heap
To spend
Spent
Spending
Post facto
There.
They will
leave their
invisible signs
Everywhere.

mammals and art

phillip baldwin

And 'above'
Is the castrating father
Who
Gives you two chances
To
Challenge his order….
And the mother?
She does too.

ALL S IS

SOME S
P

IS P

NO S

SOME
P

IS NO

mammals and art

phillip baldwin

Topography of the possible

Provisional
Plateau
Push
Being
Seeming
Not seeming
Not being
If it is Saturday
Therefore it is time
expanded
Arrows yet to divide and hit
Q.

ALL S IS P

It is Saturday
Then
Q.

Saturday or infinity
Not infinity
Therefore Saturday.

Two propositions
upon awaking
A day of paradigms…
like prayer for
The uncritical
religious
Those with real
problems with
authority.

SOME S IS NOT

SOME S IS P

My problem
Is bracing my authority
Against the day
Instead of a bearded benign
Father
Male Uber
Or earth goddess
Big with breasts and
Vescia Pieces
Big oval
Sucking back all of the pathos
Brought to those lucky to be born.

NO S IS P

Though and through I
know
The authority of this
sky father
And earth mother
By most
I fight with the
authority
Of myself
So I make a new
prayer each day
If p
Then q
P
Then
Journey.

PHILLIP.BALDWIN@GMAIL.COM

Envy? Most
believers?
Those with trouble
Holding their own
authority?
Heard animals?
Like
Most of the prayers
for believers
It is the motion
Put through the body
To hold the position
on the mesa.

ALL S IS P

Youth is between
childhood and the
adults
But, therefore,
everything is
between youth and in
it.
Days measure with
envy of the believers
who
Seem to fuel
themselves on
Animal falsity.
And every meme
makes you push your
Calculation

SOME S IS NOT

SOME S IS P

Calls
That makes you
worry
And wonder about
children
Miniature
They might be
projected
Against
Their place as
Innocent...
Against
The culpability of
adults
Who are no less
innocent
Than children

NO S IS P

The frozen
space
In time
Line
Lines of
Definite
space.

Awake
would be the
first of four
Four spaces
strung on a
day line.

PHILLIP.BALDWIN@GMAIL.COM

'hen some sort of daily hope
'hat infinite sweeps at
;ome immortality can be taken
'hen the space of decrease
;ome sort of
'oid
า
.iminal void

ALL S IS P

Then a resignation
toward but not into
sleep
For sleep
Is now that fought
thing against
information.
Floods of possible
information.
'No screens in bed',
said
The doctor.

SOME S IS NOT

SOME S IS P

The bed should be for sex or sleep
Only.
Which is wise.
But sex and sleep is that last paradigm
On the time-arrow string of the day
It floods the brain with dopamines
And the rest, perhaps, washes it out to sea.

NO S IS P

If p
Then
Q.
P: the paradigm
Then
Sleep
Or sex before sleep.
Or

PHILLIP.BALDWIN@GMAIL.COM

Six paradigms strung
Through a waking day
Like mesas, plateaus,
Above
An animal sadness
Moving and bumping
Against
A prayer-less regret.
Wash, hygiene, work, breath,
And the limbic comfort of the
other.

ALL S IS P

It is know that aesthetics
are lesser than ethics
For what is beauty but
toward a result?
And then what is action
Without a universe?
But I am a believer
Without religion
Paradigms shadow
My day
And stay.
Stay.

SOME S IS NOT

SOME S IS P

I fight my empathetic pathos for
other ground
Moving animals I have loved
Pathos
Is that between
Aesthetic
And ethic

NO S IS P

Perhaps pointing to
The high mesas of
Metaphysic.
But if it is complete
The trick is to pity
others
More than thyself
Which is wrong
Austerity
Duty
Even
P
Therefore
Q.

PHILLIP.BALDWIN@GMAIL.COM

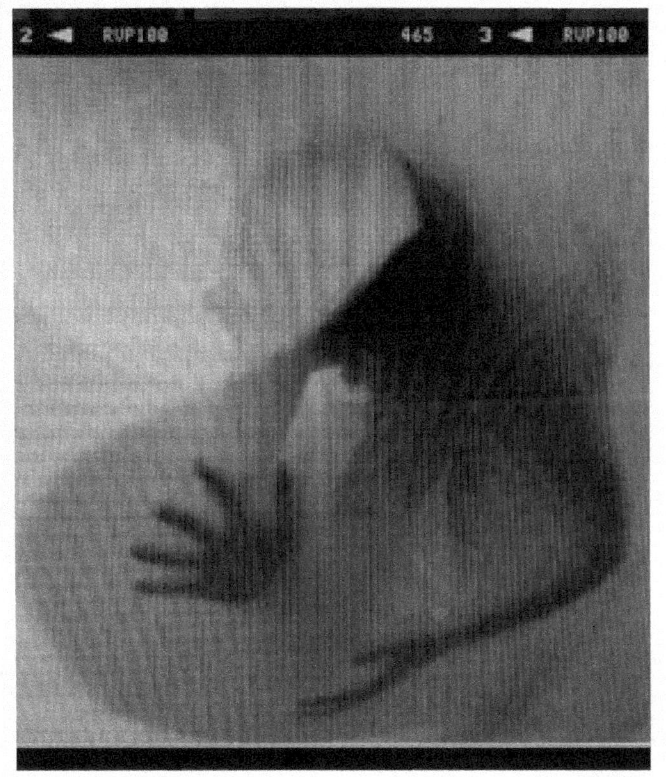

MIND-PUSH VERSE

PHILLIP BALDWIN

THE HUMANITY OF
NUMBERS

We only understand the
humanity
Of numbers through insect
behavior
Looking through the late night
milk-run
A light snow descended.
Fell in volume
Fell as volume
Fell as white pointillism
In murk city night.
Fell as a delight
And surprise

And fell as
indifference
To where I should be.
If fell as a comfort
To my warm blood
Cold city
Makes and tells me
I am more than cold
blood
Insect.
It fell as blanket to a
city
abandoned
To mystery sleep.

ALL S IS P

SOME S IS NOT

SOME S IS P

NO S IS P

Where the animal above insect
(For do insects sleep?), (dream?),
Makes their horizontal sleep
After vertical day.
The hands had become a mystery to
the savanna
Hominid: what to do with them?
I know: make most things out of
grasp.

Like the billion pointillist
snow
That never covered the
ground.
What the savanna ape
thought
With newly freed hands
Is to make happiness a
far ideal
On the horizon shore
Or the bend in the coast.
What you can't grasp
Or love at night before
sleep
Firm female for increase
Would be that thing to
throw with those

THE HUMANITY OF NUMBERS

PHILLIP.BALDWIN@GMAIL.COM

and
Dissonance within
They would throw their
pointed sorrow
For the short time
wandering.
The snow fell
Like the army flight of
winged monkey men
It came in silence
And filled the volume of
Scant free time.
Did I compulsively get late
night milk

ALL S IS P

So with hands, unsatisfied heart,
For
Compulsive coffee the next
day?
Or
Did I need it?
For I was outside
Between the insect landing at
The Wednesday bar
Doing my compulsive notes.
I look down on the passions of
insects now from winter heights
Children enter a subway
Move to the hive, which
transports them
To that museum

SOME S IS NOT

SOME S IS P

Perhaps
Or there to live
underground.
And by morning
The snow was still falling
in the gray
But it never set.
And vast human insects
make more human love

NO S IS P

To make more of their
kind.
And the children make
the hard carapace
Exterior ambition
made of
Compulsive
Plans
And occasionally
throw rotten fruit
At their son and
brother
Who woke in that form
one day?
The rest conceal it…
sniff the algorithms

BALDWIN@GMAIL.COM

Of DIY or die.
Yet most have been farmed like aphids
To secret their debt as sweet
Faith-full flow of money they never had
For years after a great war they were told
That the best they could get was that which they bought
And as they swim in the debt of birth

ALL S IS P

They make the fierce hive.
Other countries wonder
And are astonished
How high and
Steep the sides of the hive
Become to climb
And there is an unsettled hunger in the hearts
Of these

SOME S IS NOT

SOME S IS P

Who excrete junk
From
Their base holes
If happiness is the false ideal
The ghost ideal must be
The trick of suspended gratification.
And between the outer happiness they say they want
And the inner happy cognitive dissonance
Is that shell
Hard

NO S IS P

Where thoughts and hot feelings
Can ricochet around
As motive
And the two worlds become eternally separate
The only place out is
The mouth and anus
Of critical desire
'The mother's love is the only thing we can depend upon'
Said the young student.
Yet the mother has made a shell of her hard motherhood.

PHILLIP.BALDWIN@GMAIL.COM

The father is.... they
don't know.
As they wouldn't know
happiness
Only heard that is what
they
Should bring inside the
shell.
And these two warring
twins
The myth of happiness
like air/liquid

ALL S IS P

And the
suspended best
Like a cream
filling
Fight around
the exoskeleton
Of base life
Crawling
Moving

SOME S IS NOT

SOME S IS P

Not knowing which
turn to make
And slowly
consuming
Their insect
suffering
Which is dosed by
medicine or booze

NO S IS P

So that loitering
And moving
Between
consuming
And feeling
Become the
best
State of motion.

P.BALDWIN@GMAIL.COM

MIND-PUSH VERSE

PHILLIP BALDWIN

The spike in the story and the sandbox of love

The mirrored world is distinct and holds
So many peeping toms
Or so goes one version
Of the same shape, the same
Real.
Mimetic
This one takes us on the game of the line
One line
Destine to tragedy
But
A line of a life looked at.
The sandbox is the reflected world
As a game
Made

Hate each other
Yet mime the world
Which hates both.
I sit on a March day
With snow descending

ALL S IS P

SOME S IS NOT

Yet if we don't look at
these
Games who will?
If we can't look at the life
wander at
Insect like
Who will.
In some sense
We are told
That stories are like
vitamins:
So many possible good
fibers to spread out
In the 'canon'.
These two
Things

SOME S IS P

Devine nature has thrown
A big handful of cause to the
Current sandbox. The little ones deal.
All of them struggle to a Friday work place
For some reason that have to move from their
pinnacle.
The stage, the film, the sandbox is pointed
inward, to move
The base insect. What we get is identification
and empathy all
For all. The catharsis of the spike-the moment
where interest becomes fear
Is the gold of the diversion. Stories are
supposed to form but living is the open
sandbox.
Catharsis of the cowboy resolves conflicts. His
paradise...in his patriarchy...is killed off to
wander.

NO S IS P

The sandbox of oblivion play
lies below.
Who would be cured to know
that the game
Is run by the machine now? Is
it the same one who beat
Kasparov?
The big one who makes the
markets...forges the desire of
plumage
On the spiked line? 'My life
matters' says each one
holding out smart phone in the
sea of wet snow.
I like the thought of the
mirroring tiny screen
Confused by the wet dots
Before the black hole of the
subway

KED STORY AND THE SANDBOX OF LOVE

IP.BALDWIN@GMAIL.COM

Is his stage joined at the footlights?
My stage/my screen?
It makes two worlds of two same shapes
Of fitful atrocities.
Big ideas are mixed with the snow to big passions:
Fear, authority, sex, insignificance
The irrational

Like art made of vapor every
Thursday night
Where many come to care.
Is this tiny screen in the snow
outside the subway
A mimesis of the real?
What benign father looks and
knows?
Happy wet dots confuse the game
Obscure the story.
Are conflicts of the past night
resolved?
Immersed into the bad wet mirror
of the tiny screen
Tinier story?

ALL S IS P

SOME S IS NOT

SOME S IS P

NO S IS P

Do I fight with Eunuch history? That
Sandbox fingered out
For play
Of the sentient?
Peasants think it does not exist.
Is this the real gain? The real empathy of lines?
History is the real drama
Played out
Whereupon it can approach sentient change.
This one is not internal

Like the base ant confused by
snow on the
Smart screen before the ant-
hole
Author, audience, actor, action,
time, space,
They can be played on this
screen
They are told that it stands
contra history
The big machine that is.
Time is that linear thing outside
the eating machine
Markets and desire
Thanatos
Ultimate

PHILLIP.BALDWIN@GMAIL.COM

There are fingers out of the great sandbox
The snowdrift time
The confused man with mirror in hand
Wet touch obscures like his life
Before the snow and the job.
He grows, forms, dies
Ostracized
By cookie cutter slag
Out of his non-conformity.
Shakespeare is a vitamin
So we are told

From early play
'Here, form it this way…it
is eternal'.
Nothing is eternal.
Especially psychology.
Now many men stand
outside in the snow
Pecking away at tiny
screen mirrors
Trying to navigate
tragedy.
A hypotheses is to be
tested…
Can we stand outside of
the screen?
Merge with life again?

Test the future
Not loiter in the
present
Victim to the past?
Deeper real
Doesn't segment…
Those kick the
snow from their
Feet
Catharsis resolves
conflicts
That lives like
parasites
They have no role.

Then enter
The hole
And I look
down
At two
Could be a
man and
woman
And they kiss
At the
entrance
Interface
Before
parting
In the snow.

BALDWIN@GMAIL.COM

MIND-PUSH VERSE

PHILLIP BALDWIN

SHIP OF HOT SUMMERS

Heat like that of
Summers hunkered down
Only Johnny Carson
Was admitted through
To the end of the hot night
As
Presidents were
Deposed,
Wars were lost
And the three point five billion
Seemed like ten.

Now there
are seven
Going up
to eight.
Wars
chewed up
farm boys
Near
Shot
Like shish-
ka-bob
Meat
From Bell
Hueys.

ALL S IS

SOME S
P

IS P

NO S IS

SOME S
P

IS NOT P

Farm girls-
Three triplets
And seven cow maidens-
Made it to spreads in
Playboy
Penthouse
With staples in their stomachs…
Because the sleazy

Alpha
weasels
couldn't
believe
Throwing
hay bales
around
Could
make
Midwest
Blonds so
beautiful.

hip of hot summers
hillip baldwin

They were chewed up
Of sorts
Against the rocks of
Two sets of puritans
One made of their tribe
The other made
Of pedagogy.
And the vast ship of the nation
Churned on with the planet
In tow
They were lesser....
Just lost a war
To one of the smaller...
Around

In circles
Through the late hot
nights.
All hungry
All in need of that
Mammalian beauty
Of pair bonding
And pack bonding
Plural
Amped
Big
Chance now is
summer
I lecture on
Those summers of
Heat, sun,
Hay,

ALL S IS
SOME S
P
IS P

NO S
SOM
P
IS NC

Animals, and
Sequestered lives
Thirsting
To be in the
Calm eye in the biggest
City
Away for the California
Torpor.

The vicarious
lives
We now have
our
Fifteen seconds
of fame
And we hope
Facebook is
like
The seat next
to Carson.

ship of hot summers

phillip baldwin

After they struck
The underwater
object
Froze
As they couldn't
believe
The world of
Tech prosthetic
Was going down.
Sinking
Bodies would swim
Or die
Of hypothermia.
Passengers on
Great America
Would stay the course
With cardboard
comics
Like Carson
Setting a bland

We compete as the fabric
Tears
Metal strikes icebergs
The biggest tech
Goes down
Faith in the failed prosthetic
Known
To hold
Backwards
If the captains
Froze

ALL S IS

SOME S
P

IS P

NO S IS

SOME S
P
IS NOT P

But comfortable course.
Comfort food, comfort jobs,
Comfort monogamy
Taught as inert passengers
Only sending what
Authority
Could deem
Passable
Good fathers were the rule

In the line
Of gain
For alpha dudes
Settling
The vast
continent.
He was one.
You watched
many
And they drank
full.
Most of them
heavy and old

hip of hot summers

illip baldwin

ship of hot summers

phillip baldwin

Now
Comfort food
For a comfort
summer
In a land that didn't
think
Unemployment
Could hit their
Tight
Pack bonding.
Animals
Without vision

ALL S IS
SOME S
P
IS P

It didn't matter...
I could be
With myself
And summer books
And yearning to get off the next island
Tokyo, Massachusetts, Singapore,
Rome
St. Paul,
Even as I was 'in it'
Hearing the music
Like a soundtrack around...

I wanted ou
Even then
Even as they
All
Family and friends.
Attached
prosthetics
To my journey...
'Here...you will
need these.'
'The pack says you
can get these
On credit.'
Break my orbit.
Shatter it
And fly
To any shot down
island
That I have seen
A few of.

NO S
SOME
P
IS NO

I had to find the ne
launch
I knew the next or
Would cast n
Perha
To the next place it
didn't wish for
But did

At least it wasn't in
the hold
Of comfortable
Carson nights.

What is my
'rosebud'?
I have so
many
The
haunted
specter
Of youth
Is often the
only

ALL S IS
SOME S
P
IS P

NO S IS
SOME S
P
IS NOT P

Pure talisman
against
Seven billion.
Each

Having
that one
Or more
thing
Carrying
Through
a silent
ship
Of
summer
In the
dark.

ip of hot summers

ip baldwin

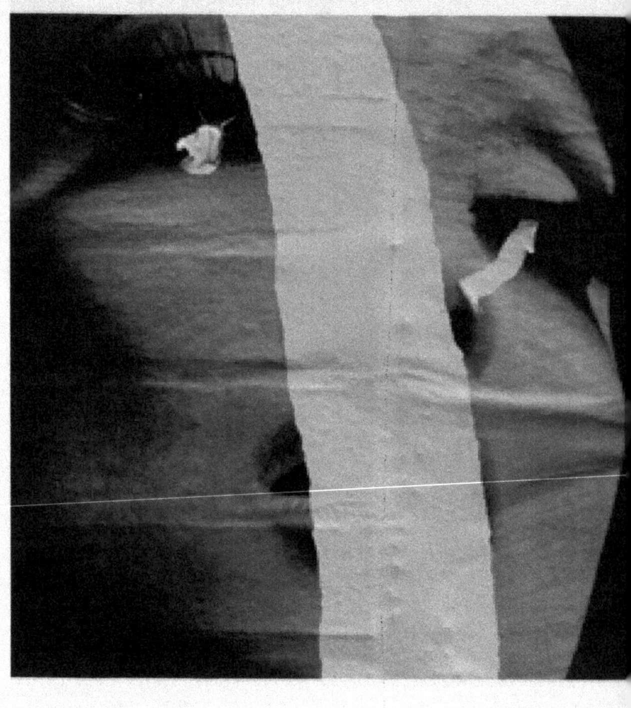

MIND-PUSH VERSE

PHILLIP BALDWIN

MAXIMUM PRESENCE

I process my late night
reflections
On
Fingers, webs, roads, alleys,
spines
Not taken.
In daydreams of these nights
I converse, question, dictate
The very clear
Intention
But know

ALL S IS P

That when I
thrust my
Thoughts
into
maximum
presence
It does
extend to
the future,
which is
not.
I think of
topographie
s

SOME S IS NOT

SOME S IS P

Walls
And the number defecated behind.
I saw the movie
Where the machine beat the
Best chess player
And the creeping fiction
That swarmed over me
Last night

NO S IS P

Was that it now
plays against
all of us.
I can imagine a
time when we
are all
quantified
By the big
market thing
All base
And only
superstructure
To keep us
hoping.

JP.BALDWIN@GMAIL.COM

It is clear as in a half dream
world
Of going to bed
And trying to muster sleep
against
Small numbers.
In my life there is no 'should
have been'
That is the biggest entitlement
Pampered
To excess

I am happy with
mere string
To make a net
to cast over
My base reality
Which isn't so
bad
As I haul in
Scant
superstructure.
But, here at
night,
The joy of
planning

ALL S IS P

SOME S IS NOT

SOME S IS P

NO S IS P

And thinking
That infinite topographies hold
Network topographies
Never paths
Yet the comfort of the
Cinema path is
That

You build the
anti-hero
The small life
inspected
Watched in a
tragic
terrarium…
That would be
nice too.
But you do it to
yourself…
You see the
cave wall and
think of
The cave wall

PHILLIP.BALDWIN@GMAIL.COM

On some
benign thing
Who will judge
your life...
imagined
Held
Hold

ALL S IS P

Topographies
of fingers
The network is
the message
And that
message is

SOME S IS NOT

SOME S IS P

Think what you need
to go to sleep
Numbers follow you
And this is no long by
humans

NO S IS P

The
noosphere is
a termite heap
With vengeful
peers
Your task is to
Dodge these
And the
machine.

IP.BALDWIN@GMAIL.COM

Recursive masks

Kepler, 1596, thought
that the best way to
explain
The harmony of the
spheres
Read 'masks',
Was to place a sphere
at the center
And then
The distance traveled
would be
Polyhedrons
To the
Fundamental Square.
Elegant

But the real
Inner
Mask to the entire universe
Was accident?
So it is
We feel
Place
Order
Chaos
And
Structure on the outside
The 'inside' is that
Thing
Known
To the observer
As will

ALL S IS

SOME S

P

IS P

NO S I

SOME

P

IS NOT

A beautiful mask
To explain
The
Position
Of sentience.

The desire
Perhaps for elegance
Perhaps
For time within time
Mass within
A void.
Perhaps.

And yet on the
street
Big is eaten by
the small
Eventually
Many
Though
And the bigger
Gatekeepers of
Self-authority
Hold gates
On the mask of
stuffed shirts
And daddy's
beatings
Learned.

death and the job/the job of death

PHILLIP. BALDWIN@gmail.com

Like the kid who was expelled
for the fist fight
With the principal
After the fight with the father
that morning
Now he flies the big planes
Turnaround.
Miraculous
Or order. Cathartic
Streamlined.
Applied like Kepler's task.
The best was to explain
heavenly bodies
Is history
Through story
To the observer
Through their mask
To another....

Through history.
To explain the future
As if physics has no
present.
The best way,
Totalizing,
To explain the limbic
Mammal
Is the present?
All present. In the heart
The rest…like the
distance Kepler explained
Is masks and
Armor

IS

S

NO S IS

SOME S

P

IS NOT P

What is love on the inside? A
sphere to square?
Or sphere to void?
Every evidence I see from a
birthday girl
To the ravages of a
Parked scooter
Erodes.
Decays
Like a masked theory
Or a language
Demanding of grammar.
Or
A sphere
Applied
To accident.

Conception to a square.
How to do things with
erosive language?
Are about accidental
attack
Yet spherical in their
inception
Like the night embraced
to conceive
From the child outward
Is the octahedron
Polyhedrons
And then to the square
Of logic death
And the parent?
The lover?

h and the job/the job of death

P. BALDWIN@gmail.com

Recursive masks
Inward as outward.
The consuming
student is worried
about
Themselves.
As product
As device

As the commodity of
Critical thought they have
to embody
Petulant
As if the new interlocutor
Is a gatekeeper?
To their bliss
To their perfect credit
rating
Like stupid GPAs....
Eaten away by tiny,
banal, evil, predators
Is where the bully lives.
The numbers
Mask

ALL S IS

SOME S

P

IS P

NO

SO

P

IS

The stuffed shirt
The quarterback
Alpha
To all
Myth
Of the world
As harmonic spheres
Perhaps the best language
Like
PC talk.
But
Bites
Eats
Erodes
Corrodes...

In the bites like small
sharks
And smaller piranha,
This is where the mask of
embrace
Every night
Expands and explains
In Kepler's language
Why there is so much
elegance.
God does not mask
Nor
Yes, or
Yes
'He' does play dice with
the universe
And
Sometimes he throws it
where
Nobody can see it.

death and the job/the job of death

PHILLIP. BALDWIN@gmail.com

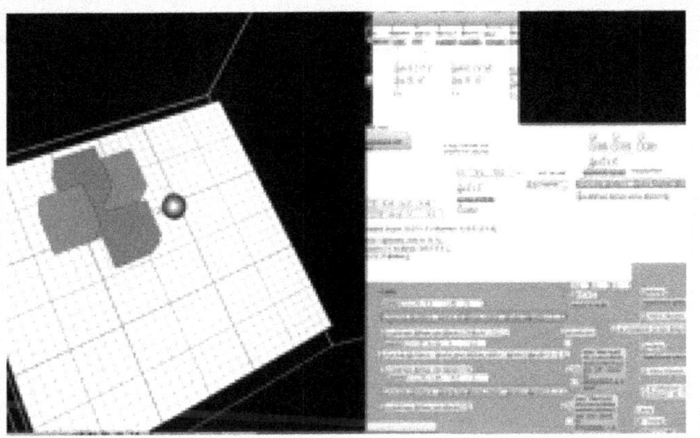

MIND-PUSH VERSE

PHILLIP BALDWIN

Tree line

At the distance of a
lucid dream I
Saw a line of trees
Across a wide field
There I couldn't tell if
the sky was gray
For
Every tree was the color
of autumn.
I was happy to see this
in a distance.
It was happiness that I
felt so I kept
This through the day.
Happy was not an ideal
For ancients
Perhaps it was the
aesthetic real: the ethic
Was spelled out like a
law...eats or be eaten.

When there are debates about
everything else
The local meal rules supreme.
But this tree line dream...
This was not about possession
Or fickle people
This was
A line of trees on the near
horizon.
As I rolled the simple image
Around
I did not know if it was cold or
warm
If it was cloudy or sunny

We, modern, worry
about the dynamic of
this
Ethic

Perhaps it was a little of all
of these
As pain is a language
The cure might be an
image
Not the other way around
I do not wait for the
salience of pain
I have seen so much of
cookie cutter
Archetypes
Pulled asunder
Sex wrapped in the
authority
Of the future moments
Daddy's approbation
Toward the respect of
jezebels.
The idea that we work to
live...
We live to work

Not as aesthetic compulsion
But to stay as the red queen:
in one place.
Youth before the tree line is,
perhaps
Taking yourself out of the
fecund
Forgetful moment
To obey
Like hunting pack animals...
The pleasures of defying the
dog
Or a trip into the fold
Of ten million ants.
I cut the edges of the cookie
cutter
For a real adult is one who can
Live before suspended
gratification
Yet ride it....

PHILLIP.BALDWIN@GMAIL.COM

One who
reaches
into twenty
years of
twisting
mistakes?
But one
who plumbs
two million.
But what do
I look at?
When I hate
the
infantilized
script?
The
college, the
car, the
wife, the
house, the
kid, the
divorce?
Straight
from the
bank's
script.

If you stay it is in the
dissatisfied present.
I found I needed a
personal language for
pleasure
Sex became quantity
For it is hard to
remember
Kinesthetic bliss.

And pain I know I should fear
And empathy should be for
the right thing:
Not another's pain to
sublimate yours
Humanity in the anthill is less
about ethics
For the hive is
Obvious to all
It is

Moreover
About
When
The hinged image
A line of colored trees
Close in scope
Far
To see
A private language
To me.

LIP.BALDWIN@GMAIL.COM

THERE ARE SMALL THINGS THAT EAT
YOU ALIVE IN THE HEAT

It is the 'big other'...I have found...
Long since every morning's wake
When I saw all my boots
Leather bags
Covered with mildew
On the edge of the
Jungle in Singapore.
Half measures
Don't work
You must attend to the
Dead things that are the skin
Of the dead every day.

And the live one with a
trigger.
The heat brings out
The efficient eating.
Those who
Have spent their lives in
Bench warming
Alpha weasels
Hoards like mildew
On dead leather
Where even stuffed linen
Had that smell in the
deepest closets.
Insects

ALL S IS
SOME S
P
IS P

Small things
Like my old,
ugly bike
Stolen
On a hot
weekend.
The dark park
was filled with
A protest march
About a racist
Or perceived
racist
Murder trial.
Like Roshomon,
Not many where
there
Except the dead

Specialize
And they over come
any attack

NO S
SOM
P
IS N

On their 'being'
In time
Dasein
As the grand
narrative of grand
survival
Overlaps with the
single gestures
Of eating what is at
hand

there are small things that eat you in the heat

phillip baldwin

While the
enemy
sleeps.
Sex and
desire move
the city
That is what
all which to
over look
Like bad
fashion of
twenty years
before.
As they now
live in an
invisible era
Of
Good
fashion
invisible

Like vermin who
eat at you
Bike thieves
Racial encounters
at
The molecular
level
With 'grand
theories' and
ontologies
Of what that race
really is...
This is it.
Before they are
eaten
And grow wisdom
and cancer
And age
And toxic food
The small eat
you...against the
grain.
With the grain
Like movies eat
books

Why not?
This is making and
consuming

ALL S IS
SOME S
P
IS P

NO S IS
SOME S
P
IS NOT P

Because they are 'compact'
With the arch of Aristotle.
And pecking cell phone
artists
Shoot cities with filters
That instantly makes them
1920's savants.

As opposed to
gelling in
Front of a tube.
Where does the time
come from?
Dasein
The time between.
Make yours now
Before you are
eaten.

ere are small things that eat you in the heat

ip baldwin

Time and being

Past the sun
And the breeze on the beach...
Past the sun's arch
And the time it takes
To think that your body
Will rebel in stages.
Even now
Healthy...
Past the entropy
Of the
Cosmic bang
Sending out toward
The big crunch
Past the fragments
Of close individuals
Timeless
Repeat
Repeat
How they will say the same things
And how you will try to save them
As on a lifeboat
In the middle
Of a sea between
Ubiquity
And anonymity.
How sweet they smelled
How deep their trance eyes in full
Ecstasy
How they looked up at you
And thought
This is
The alpha and omega of passion
Of pleasure
Of things that don't scatter from the big bang
To the corners as live as dead stones
In cold
Cosmos.
They look up in sweat:
Never leave, always protect,
Always be here so that
When the big crunch occurs
We are holding fast.
Together.
Like the time I was four
And saw awful news on the
Tube...and turned to my mother:
I want to be buried with you.
Now I have enough

PHILLIP.BALDWIN@GMAIL.COM

Of the navigator
Viking raider…
What is cast out is touched by thought
The big crunch of being close
Yet far
Like my cancer infused brother
Saying
'Goodbye' nine months before he did
And nine minutes before he saw me last.
If everyone
Who was that intimate?
Ripped
As they, the female looked in your eyes and said:
Never leave me to the big crunch
For the exploding universe has made me so lonely.
You saw
Ok…take it easy
Be mad at economics
Not yourself
If you have to pray only pray
For the wind in the sails that you made
And hoisted
And for the times
We
Are in our big crunch
Deep inside each other
We are not cast far as dead
Sentient flowers
Into cold corners
But tucked
In a sailors warm night
On the beach.

IP.BALDWIN@GMAIL.COM

ENHANCES

I look down from my
window
And know
That half these insects will
be harvested
By 'the other' they let
Into
Their small
Rooms

REVERSES INTO

Beach walks
Broken hearts
Misaligned geometry

ALL S IS

SOME S

P

IS P

NO S I

SOME

P

IS NOT

RETRIEVES

Small women
Making smaller daughters
Like enviable fragments
Of their selves.
Benchwarmers...
Desire cooked with
authority:
All of this is the scampering
Half selves to be
Stuck to 'another'
In intimacy.

OBSOLESCES

And there they will eat upon
the carcass
Of the whole
2.8 times is the spoken
language
Than social grooming of the
fur.
Of that it must be at least
another three times
The written language is
Against the onslaught
Of anonymity
Anomie
And
A crumpled death
Brought to life again
through
Writing.

PHILLIP. BALDWIN@gmail.com

ENHANCES

So we look for dusty
archives
In the vast cloud
Of efficient social grooming.
Rogue elements nip
And chew and the weak...
they can smell out
Survival patterns
Not in place.

REVERSES INTO

In the stew of the morning
You can think and dream
both
Of what you have to do to
surmount
These...
Why has this upright animal
Become so reptilian?
Why
Do zombies figure
Well in every sense of
entertainment
For

LL S IS

OME S

P

NO S IS

SOME S

P

IS NOT P

RETRIEVES

'The cinema'...saying, as it
does
That soon the base value of
life will be filled with a
Landscape of the undead?
Those who don't care if they
are harvested.
Not awake like the Buddha.
'Expression' is the little
pretty stones
In the jewel-box homes.

OBSOLESCES

But yet
Biking girls, down there, are
beautiful.
Earnest, urban...making
their claim of the
Piranha-swarm center.
And fits, they move
The others
Over
The hard ground breathing
carbon air.
For it is better...and
Baudelaire said: city air
makes you free.

ography of a point

LIP. BALDWIN@gmail.com

ENHANCES

Down there pounding hard
pavement
Are those disappointed by
The surrounding few
Heartbreak
Anger

REVERSES INTO

Misalliance.
Authority is the engine of
their desire.
Down there.
And

ALL S IS

SOME S

P

IS P

NO S I

SOME

P

IS NOT

RETRIEVES

Jealous benchwarmers
Snipe
And authority
Sets liquid desires
And blame

OBSOLESCES

Is always placed on the
copulating parents
For not knowing the time
they through
Progeny into.
For soon I must go pay my
rent for
The time I made
Standing still.

topography of a point

PHILLIP. BALDWIN@gmail.com

IN ANNUAL BEING BECAME

TROUBLED SLEEP BUT LUCKY.
Lucky to be here
After my parents made love…there are something's
Left for the privacy of the verse maker
Every five-meter line to hit…
Why five?
Why not fifty-four?
Bad sleep from a cold
But healthy beyond
My years
Robust…
Not knowing
If the bigger questions of being
Being as
Enslavement
As
The metaphysics of comparison
Is held up to a life…something.
This is it.
I hold it up to happiness
Yet know
Existence is finite
Poems are cheap when
Dashed upon a page,
Prayers are more profound
When they don't repeat liturgy.
So I spill
On this my day.
Language is that thing that unmakes the animal
In men
And women.

It is that thing that allowed for 2.8 times better
Social grooming in human apes…
Where you don't have to pick upon alphas.
I did and do flood myself with texts
To push back the bestiality in me.
Now we have arenas, have radio, have TV
And have the burrow holes of the Internet.
The beast that is more than animal comes out.
We are the rational animals to know we are not
And animal
At all.
And our language…even my language to myself
To understand it is my birthday…
Knows that
At my being is language

P.BALDWIN@GMAIL.COM

We should sit
And listen to this
As hard as that is

It is a gift.
So I will try today.
On my birthday
To do just that.

PHILLIP.BALDWIN@GMAIL.COM

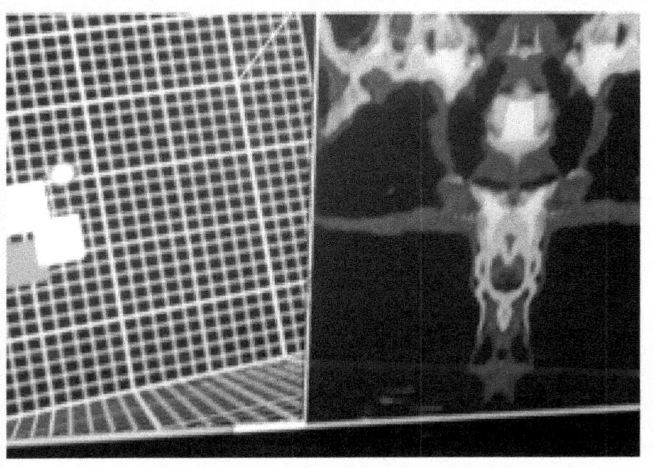

MIND-PUSH VERSE

PHILLIP BALDWIN

ENHANCES

Stupefaction

To make yet to make
Some
Micro
Walk
Micro narrativeOf the past...
memory

Full
Like a blunted
Edged carving

REVERSES INTO

To follow
To feed-back
Feed back
Feed

ALL S IS
SOME S
P
IS P

NO S I
SOME
P
IS NOT

RETRIEVES

To thirst
To thirst for more than
image
To
Remember
To remember to thirst

OBSOLESCES

To desire
To desire more than
memory
Where most
Fear the future
You desire it

micro narrative
PHILLIP. BALDWIN@gmail.com

ENHANCES

Most think that
It would take
A degree of less
To live in and for the future.
What is it?
In the regrets
There
To get old.

REVERSES INTO

Not saying what you feel
Not doing what is/was
passion
Working too much
On that which is
Pointless.

LL S IS

OME S

S P

NO S IS

SOME S

P

IS NOT P

RETRIEVES

Not making more friends
Not having more/deep
Lovers
Top
Things
Not
Having
The gall
To

OBSOLESCES

Put material as mere fuel
And passion as essence

This is
Bottom
To not
Have seen
To
The detail
Of the past…memory

cro narrative

LIP. BALDWIN@gmail.com

ENHANCES

Full
Like a blunted
Edged carving
Or
Rapid prototyped
Dream
That
Is the
Middle
For remembrance
To understand
The sustained

REVERSES INTO

Public
To have fought
For ideals
To have come
Under the radar
Of the mediocre

ALL S IS

SOME S

P

IS P

NO S IS

SOME

P

IS NOT

RETRIEVES

Inept frauds
But very apt frauds
Who know their job as
frauds?
And criminals

OBSOLESCES

Who would have
sequestered
The entire planet
Chained to their hot water
heater
In the basement.

PHILLIP. BALDWIN@gmail.com

Often the only thing you can do
Is write
When the world eats everyone around
It is feeding on the best
And the
Most weak.
How could they make the grade?
How could they survive?
Beasts?
How could they
Make it when the
Houses raise
Up
And they say the market
Is full?
How could they get gouged?
By their neighbor?
How could they
Hold
Enough
Hard steel
Point
Help
On them
Knowing
The day full
Knowing
Not the sunlight
Of earlier days?
How could they not know
The
Juice
Of the journey?
And
Remember
The bight
Challenge of love
In each day?
How could they not know
That there should be something
Other
Than quantity
Holding human bodies to earth
So-not like ants-the fly
Up to the thin air and then
Burst into flame.
What do we have that comforts now?
Out of the cold?
What do we have that doesn't make
The brother pay dearly?

where..all you

ALDWIN@GMAIL.COM

What do we have but
Sibling
Avalanche
And other
Redress for
Full transduction?
What do we have that remains
Except these words
In some server in the sky?

Going native in the point cloud

IDEA – the concept or impetus behind the services being offered:

Ideas of the destiny: the path. Overland. 'Fun is standard, the road, optional.'
Said the ad.
I propose that all
Endeavors
End before they begin
And the tired ideas of individuality
Push
Some collective
Not 'natural'. Werd.
Werden…
Becoming, of some group of artist-maker-earners…. everyone
Could see their 'History' like a hill in Vietnam: it grinds to meat.
And every aspect of the 'natural'
Took some five minutes of fame…
From all…
It would be
Very compelling
If every one
Of the seven billion (not knowing the top number as a given)
Would be compelling like a lamp
To a bug…
Too interesting…
Because they have taken
History
Like a jungle hill
And turned it into some sort of 'authentic' clay
For interest…attention…
And we would demand that everybody look…
Have to…
Like the hill
In Tennessee.

PRACTICE – the effectiveness of how the services are put into practice and the impact they have on the artistic community:

Devise some clay-history
That every single seven billion….
No matter the thick ignorance
Could form and
Transform
Alchemy

JP.BALDWIN@GMAIL.COM

With thei
Dasei
In place

'What do you propose to make that so?'
Said you.
It would take some skill
Of course learning
Reading papyrus scripts
Rosettas of debt.
Disabuse all of the idea they owe
Anybody else.
Fundamental
Waking of the fish from the sea
Who couldn't see the sea?
'The modern' wasn't like this...
It smell of new car.... something not bad...
But didn't smell of the sweat and toil
Of living
Like
In fluids
Ground on a hill. So make it something
That fits in an upright hand.

DEVELOPMENT – the contribution the services make to the development of the arts and cultural community in the state:

After this magic
(If you can repeat it, it is a science)
Give some lump of this
Half soft, wet, wetness.
To all
Part hard, hardness
And ask them
To all, old and child,
To hold it like themselves.
It is.
Authentic...
And say thrice: 'from now on, we don't consume, we produce.'
Of course it might dry before then
So you must keep it wet
With any part of your wet body you think: authentic.
Surface not shiny.... mud...
Being...beyond becoming...
In hand yet destiny
Dirty yet fine...
Never ashamed of the wetness
Of time
Returning.
This is

BRAIN TO DANCE/CAVE TO SHADOWS

PHILLIP.BALDWIN@GMAIL.COM

Not a thing that takes time
Away from your precious, distracted time.
It is time.
Mirror. Reflect
In mud back to you…
End of your being all bits
Like an idea of your death
Or your death at holding thus.
Gnostic, agnostic prayer for the holding
Of
Something that helps you
Rid yourself
Of creditors.

CONTEXT – the context in which the services are being offered:

And with this, wet, hard, transformed…you remember
All those complicated things
That happened with Chinese medicine:
too much Yin
Means
Calling of Yang…

And
Never, don't,
Place it down
Wet, dry, or transformed
Without wishing it to be
Like your life
Beyond destiny
So that
It is…
Becomes…
Makes
The most obscure corners
Whole.

Place it there
As you would yourself…never forget.
And
Repeat
Seven billion times….
Empathy.

IP.BALDWIN@GMAIL.COM

With their
Dasein
In place.

'What do you propose to make that so?'
Said you.
It would take some skill
Of course learning
Reading papyrus scripts
Rosettas of debt.
Disabuse all of the idea they owe
Anybody else.
Fundamental
Waking of the fish from the sea
Who couldn't see the sea?
'The modern' wasn't like this...
It smell of new car.... something not bad...
But didn't smell of the sweat and toil
Of living
Like
In fluids
Ground on a hill. So make it something
That fits in an upright hand.

DEVELOPMENT – the contribution the services make to the development of the arts and cultural community in the state:

After this magic
(If you can repeat it, it is a science)
Give some lump of this
Half soft, wet, wetness,
To all
Part hard, hardness
And ask them
To all, old and child,
To hold it like themselves.
It is.
Authentic...
And say thrice: 'from now on, we don't consume, we produce.'
Of course it might dry before then
So you must keep it wet

With any part of your wet body you think: authentic.
Surface not shiny.... mud...
Being...beyond becoming...
In hand yet destiny

PHILLIP.BALDWIN@GMAIL.COM

Dirty yet fine...
Never ashamed of the wetness
Of time
Returning.

This is
Not a thing that takes time
Away from your precious, distracted time.
It is time.
Mirror. Reflect
In mud back to you...
End of your being all bits
Like an idea of your death
Or your death at holding thus.
Gnostic, agnostic prayer for the holding
Of
Something that helps you
Rid yourself
Of creditors.

CONTEXT – the context in which the services are being offered:

And with this, wet, hard, transformed...you remember
All those complicated things
That happened with Chinese medicine:
too much Yin
Means
Calling of Yang...

And
Never, don't,
Place it down
Wet, dry, or transformed
Without wishing it to be
Like your life
Beyond destiny

I TO DANCE/CAVE TO SHADOWS

ALDWIN@GMAIL.COM

So that
It is...
Becomes...
Makes
The most obscure corners
Whole.

Place it there
As you would yourself...never forget.
And
Repeat
Seven billion times....
Empathy.

PHILLIP.BALDWIN@GMAIL.COM

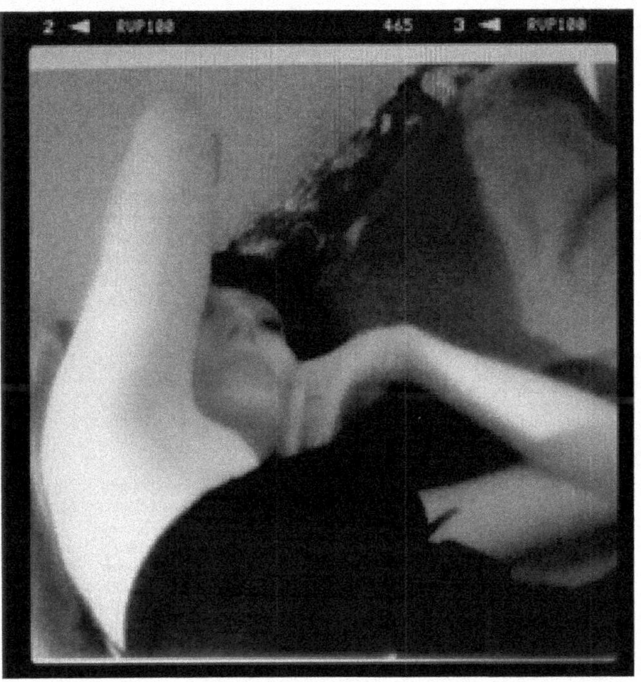

MIND-PUSH VERSE

PHILLIP BALDWIN

Dream of the dream hotel

In relentless rain
Wet city
I awoke to sun
And the fresh summer
Remembering my dreams

This one was of a chase
And levels of skill inside
Some
Endeavor.

I think it was a chase for money
Or moreover a living
And, of course, the number of
adventures
You could have
Trying to earn a living.

It was in the deep jungle
Call and response
And how the vast hotels peaked above
The rain
And fog
When the rain subsided.

I was following
Some Mid Eastern student
Through
The hotel looking for the trail
We had to take then fly
Out to the next place this elusive job
Went

Though
The hotel
El Amitar
Seemed a paradise
In the afternoon sun after a jungle rain
As it was surrounded by swimming pools
And impossibly mysterious women
within.

I follow my head through the pictures
Nay, environments
That gets projected without a source
Real but not
The generate

PHILLIP.BALDWIN@GMAIL.COM

Over
A sweet regret in the dream
Perhaps laying down clues
To paths I should take now
Like a cave dream
With roads spurting from the wakeful sides.

What does it mean to chase like a criminal
A job
Let land in a paradise hotel
Wishing for a stasis?
What does it mean
To take...
As I do now
Trusting words after I trust
My impressions of the sleep...
Roads out of a definite nowhere
And the roads really mean something.
So many forks in a backward consideration
I wouldn't take
Yet I do not regret the taking
Because I did have the
Gift
Of space/time...
I trusted
That
The journey was delicious
Leaving was regret
But
The hint of un-weighted efficiency for the next
Move
Was the best
Way
To bourgeon
My constant youth
Toward finding the fork.
...Of course as I now did in this jungle hotel
Miles away from snowy origin.
How detailed is a dream
If only by atmosphere
Many pixels it teaches
As is still
Almost pry you out of artifice.
What simple technology within?
I told them all to sit at their evening's bed
(Even if they all slept alone)
And stare at their hands in calm...
Then, in the ancient tech dream

JP.BALDWIN@GMAIL.COM

They would pull their hands out
And move with will over the forks-in-the-road
There.... enjoy the dream with will
Lucidly.

Yet I must trust
All it in even all
The projection of the sleep
And trust
That even in the chase of
A job

I should enjoy where I am at
The best
Out of hard jungle rain
Making delicious sunsets
Arrived at Paradise.

PHILLIP.BALDWIN@GMAIL.COM

The interpretation of dreams

I dreamt=I think for the second night running=that
I was King Lear in an elaborate production
Of King Lear.
It was implicit that I should get the role
Amongst dozens of people working on the production
And one of my corpulent old professors from
Undergrad days
Was the director.
The gossamer scrim set
Was moved up and down a gym
And the whole
Cast, crew, and support
Had to live on the set.
We kept moving our clothing
And parts of our
Valuable existence
Such as laptops and cell phones.

The gossamer set
Would move up and down the gym,
And the tech
Crew had that
Arrogant
Technocratic
Myosis
About all of them.
I would come up to the professor and ask: when do we rehearse?
No answer.
I had a feeling that
There would be no rehearsal
Only a performance.

It seemed to be endless preparation
Toward the end
I was the end
As a Lear without lines
Memorized.

I thought that I should view this
Then improvise
Forget the precise memes
Of
400-year-old speech.
I should move about the dark
Gym

.BALDWIN@GMAIL.COM

And the dozens
Of support staff
Like Bunraku

Operators
In a type
Of river town
There was a type
Of delicious darkness

And prepare to play
The fool
King who
Would give it away
Knowing that none of the techies
Would know what is going on
With the language
They just knew it was good for them.
This was the sequel to my dream
From the night before
As I lie preparing.

Purity of history
In quadrants.
Geometry
Of
Equal sides
And volumes.... syllogisms
Every anxiety

To all of the prepara
And my things...the things I c
On my back in the
Would get separ
And miss
I would stick them on my b

The fat profe
Had a kind of
Of prepara
I liked its pu

Of prepara
Felt like it was leadin
The best existe
Performance I could h

Even if it was improv.

But the lines…didn't they all come here for the lines?
To listen to
The eternal suffering
Of foolish
Forks in the road?
Moves that

Were not supposed to be?
Risk literacy
From the center
The tiny center.
Of individual
Proportion
And desire?

Between preparing?
There is nothing?
Who would the audience be?
But the staff?
Those who swarmed around you
Perhaps waiting for you to 'fail'
Would you not
Absorb
The ancient words
Though

And the light scrim
Set
Kept moving…
The dark bodies kept
Mulling

I wondered how I was to
Memorize my lines…
And the
Fork in the road
Production
Of King Lear
Spilled out
Into the river town…

And I
Listened to the cold June rain
In a half sleep
To wallow
In
A possible
Murk reading
Of my fate.

LIP.BALDWIN@GMAIL.COM

SYMBOLO

FAMILY
FRAGMENTS:
GENERATIVE PIECE

SYMBOLO
Was Aristotle's term
Taken from
The Symposium
'Tally'...
An account
Of another world.

Stand as another world
Where 'money' was
Something to be broken
in half
Like the payment for
dinner or meeting.
Then reconstituted.
So many fragments
Bits

ALL S IS

SOME S

P

IS P

NO S IS

SOME

P

IS NOT

To
Pay...
Does the world owe
us a debt?
To be born?
That fat chance
Of will
Or just
Naked
Luck
Desire?

How many broken bits
need to come off...
For another meeting?
What is owed to those
thrust into
Consciousness?
Blinking in the dark
Cause blinking is all
They have
Not/never prepared for
The blinding
Yellow sun...

SYMBOLO

Can we take a clay flute
Long with music
Tone,
Key
And keep breaking it
In hopes of the next meeting?
Then
The low bass turns to treble
To high soprano.

We never have luck with
those things
Except to
Place them
With that/those
Shards from chance
scarlet friends

.L S IS
OME S
P

NO S IS
SOME S
P
IS NOT P

Some on the middle
of
The clay flute
Some seldom
touching the blue lips
And when this is

Reassembled
With the most
Dire throat-clenched
Hope
Oxygen...
Then
The wind
With spring wetness
Takes it to
Tone again.

'MBOLO

MAGICAL VAPOR

Rolls of my coffee
In the cool humid morning.
It disappears into
The space of
My day's intention.
What gives, as I smell half trees?
In windows there are those rising?
And
Gridding the day
Late already.
The rush to the subway below
And prepare for a life of indebtedness.
Or are underway.
What I owe the most are
Coins to my sleep
In preparation for the last
Blinking
Not in pain...nobody hopes
For protracted pain
Over wet afternoons
In bed
Where food, like shelter and
Family are not entitled.
The worst they can expect
Is that it lingers out across the
Last bit of life
And that the others should see
Their personal apocalypse.
Two worlds meet in the middle
Meet each other in obsolescence.
A third place now is begged for
Across
As two plates collide
And crush
Willful bad habits underneath
To stream
A fluid will issue out
Of the magical world
Were flogging the bad river
Is in place,
And the perspectival
Hunger for the infinite still gathers.
Cars groan below
The bodies grow fat with bad food.
They can't think early morning thoughts
Without that

PHILLIP.BALDWIN@GMAIL.COM

Of fleeing
Just before
Their suspicion of their frailties.
Cool air makes magic vapor
On

And above
Across it. Spending.
Showing,
Itself before
Spreading out in thin air.

BALDWIN@GMAIL.COM

THE DUST OF EONS AND THE MORNING OF SPRING

The dust of eons has fallen
And I pick it up in my small abode.
It is past annoyance
And my future.
I see it now
To get rid of it
To
Stop
And wonder if
I only breathe
The worst
Of decay
And I
Should
Fight it
As I flies
Outside in
Millions of year
Exhaust expunged.
I feel the
Generous sun
After a
Hard winter
Hustled
Where I breathe
And look down on
A full artery of traffic.
Ancient faces
Of Ptolemaic Egypt
Hold the key to unlock
Why faces hold
The easier life for
The future children.
Why a face?
Why not a full body
As in
Vintage Playboy?
To think that some
Of these ladies
Are now dust
Not gathered but lost
Is most of the part of beauty.
But the face
Left in the tired ideas
Of the perspectival vacuum...
Is the last thing not shattered into
Thousands of points
Where everybody fights
The past, present, and future
Of dust

PHILLIP.BALDWIN@GMAIL.COM

With the online
Magazine of how
They are doing in their
Struggle against dust.
When the wet lungs
No longer breath
But they
Themselves have
Turned to dust
The roman roads
Of Internet lines
Hope to hold
So that
The cult of fifteen minutes
Of fame
And not frustrated young
White men with guns
Finds an apt staving of dust
And the attention that
Every Alberti wished to fight for
Is gone
So that the dust in the grid,
Handfuls hiding in small rooms
On throbbing thoroughfares
Is that enemy the face fights
In a floating world
Of ancient
Webs
To micro-modern
And placing 'now'.

We consist of cords stuck to screens

Feed us
As we walk over the lands of being alone
And feed our screens…
Mostly.
Energy is that thing we both have
Both need
Though our energy is a mystery
And power
Is to our cords
Is
Something each child knows about
Nickel cadmium batteries
How long,
How to train,
How far they have to travel over
The lunar
Expanse of the
Faustian perspectival
Cone
Sucking in curiosity
Vomiting
Consumer petulance.
Infinity consist
Not in
Quantities of air
Or the hopeless nothing
Outside the atmosphere
Or the philosophy of
The space station.
Umbilical mother-born whelps:
Half wishing to be whipped
After shitting
Again…
They don't journey to the wild anymore
Within that flat shiny plate
In which a faux meal is waiting
In which they can avoid the boring,
Thus being boring.
It is in the gesture
Of the plug
How to get one at a deli
Or airport
And not to tap into
The connection with
The loved one
The intimate
But with
Other snide consumers
Who place the screen over
What bores them

WE CONSIST OF CORDS STUCK TO SCREENS

PHILLIP.BALDWIN@GMAIL.COM

And invests it with diversion...
Like the binoculars of
Seething real
Frames
Over grace and hope
As Fra Angelico
Would have it: or Alberti.
There is sophistication with many
Frames
Past, present, future...
But no grace of the glue
Of time
An edge event to all.

Far point: log out, turn off.
Messy bits of the shattered real
That really eats flesh
Not attached to a battery.
Energy
To hope of vengeance
Stuff a harmonica in the mouth
Of a sadistic consumer
That you once knew
Consumer her life
In tidier evil bits
Chunks of your life
That she could edit
To fit-cut and paste-in a Gnostic
land
It is your bit
That is removed
And you have returned
To the moon
To stuff that harmonica in.
'Remember this screen?'
Fade.

LIP.BALDWIN@GMAIL.COM

TOPOGRAPHY OF GNOSTIC HILLS

Catching the last of cold spring dream
Perhaps it is one dream
Spread over a lifetime.
Look for the authentic self
With the place firm
In dasein.
Look for fat female
Graduate students
Who think they have found

The hide ou
For there
Tepid souls
To hide
Never hic
Behind the prosthetic
Of technis
How it places time
Behind and before

Never within.
How do I take the elements of the day
That now bridezilla does
Who thinks
The journey is the ritual
Who think that a man as vanishing point
Will take care of the rest of her life
To replicate the Oedipal whole
Infinite 'Werden' is done
And where they wake up surprised to find
That sex is the most important navigation
To their humble hubby.
The journey is
Not the ritual that cleanses
Both binaries
In repression or ritual.
So the Dasein of one big dream
Is punctuated by waking
Into assumed hells
Of non-authenticity.

'Men' are the reason these
Fat fakes use
To cloud their authentic
Authority
In Dasein.
Mine?
I've got mine

To leave the bricks of every second
To throw myself toward a vanishing point
Gnostic hell is a type of awareness

PHILLIP.BALDWIN@GMAIL.COM

Perhaps guilt
That you could have run
The course differently
Even though you have run it
Or are yet to run.
Anger as a being
The baddast thang

Breath in to practice
What it means
To have every being
Met.
To have
Stupendous caverns
To fall into.
Craters
Not to get caught
In inauthentic
Being of
Da man: larger ice traps
That ensnares one
Even with the most sincere
Illusion that dead in an imagined life
Without time
Only paths
And posing,
Grinding,
Maya not only is: it makes,
Projects,
Replicates,
Repeats.
You can come upon a pocket of them
As you climb
Some mountain
Invisible.
Dream a Gnostic dream of 'out'.
Spark of spark....
This is the path:
Even as you fly overhead
As in a series of uninterrupted dreams
Like Bridzilla
Who thinks she can use sex as a weapon
On one guy throughout her life
If her feminist terrain doesn't go well.
Now we can see everybody
Nay here comes everybody,
In a reptilian dream
Of the inauthentic.
Anything to shirk making
The authority

No matter how small
Of the becoming self.
Everybody
Has exploded
With

The
Cause
Of film
Short
Pictures
Like Masaccio's
Pieta.
Or Youtube films
Where everybody has Authority.
Being
Is in fifteen minutes
Being is
Plastered
In breezy magazine-style

Feeds
Being
Is complaining
Like a scammed consumer
After the fact
Shirking the
Result
Of producing
Dasein.

MIND-PUSH VERSE

PHILLIP BALDWIN

PUNCTURING INFINITE SPACE

Entitled like any of these brats
More of the smell of milk on them
Every year...
They not only need policing
They thirst for it.
Passion is that thing
That spreads out like a sky
And a path
And where you hope to
See a dome of the
Heavens above
But not.

Most of them
Are afraid of the infinite space
Beyond their indifferent parents
Molds of them
Breed
Be obedient
More learned
Spent
And then their public teachers are like
Police
Of knowledge
When it is all around them
Passion for them is an escape
Into a tundra
Where you don't leave the camp
Or the lower chakras.
They need the drink
Mostly
To 'know'.

'Werd' is weird.
Becoming for them
Destiny into infinite space
Perspectival of all
Of
That is formed
From the great Tuscan cities
Planned
To be viewed from two
Magic lines of destiny:
The ground plane line
And the horizon.
Above that is a dot
That emerged within one of these
cities
Perhaps when it was
In the dark

PHILLIP.BALDWIN@GMAIL.COM

Perhaps under siege.
And out of the primitive
Then mythic morass came
The perspectival life.
Floating about these two lines
Where ever you look...
Gunpowder, printing, and
Double entry accounting.
Two, then third implied.
But, perhaps now
All is done
Ideas spent
Like wrapping
Caesars and machines emerge
The young are entitled to the same
Faux material lives
Of their parents
Without the risk.
Born into debt we still are
Indebted to the
First woman who made
Leavened bread.
And the car.
Him
Who made that.
And use
Our brats
Still see the point above
The two lines
And they hope they risk
That they will like where
They punch the hole...
Into infinite space.

LIP.BALDWIN@GMAIL.COM

Calling out to the
other twenty feet
away:
Can you believe
that?
I see it too above the
grasslands
Hold onto a stick, an
ax, and a camera
I see it
As I jump the
possible portals

I believe it because I can hold it
And throw my voice to you
And for all the theories of the
alienated
This is true: I can now make of meal
of what I see in wonder.
I can stay on the plane
Or I can move
And grip

ALL S IS

SOME S

P

IS P

NO S I

SOME

P

IS NOT

Disentangled dreaming
The hand touches the model earth of
your skin
Opens your mouth to fit
Sense of the moving world
And your accommodating pelvis
And what was vertical becomes
Purely
Horizontal
Best trope for any
For many
Times we will move again
Assessing it before slumber.

And share with thrown voice
I can touch you
Before the sun goes down.
And we can recount the day
In the horizontal
Before sleep
Before

GENERATIVE POEM OF THE SQUARE

PHILLIP BALDWIN

LAND OF LAYERED HISTORY

I read
Far into the night
Of jungle battles
Of farm boy gunners
From
Doors of
Hueys.
As farm mothers worried
So did my own
Of them
And their
Safety
In a body-count industrial war.
How much this is like the kid
Who road in a tank
And plowed through Fallugia
Industrial production
And dumping on some poor country
That they think can't stand up for itself.
Always
Blowback in the city
Sunny day of the millions of kite papers
Over Brooklyn heights
As the two building came down.

We assume, like the middlebrow, middle class
Mothers
That there were fronts.
There were none.
And they came close to
Us in the states
Layers
And jungle mountains are high
And full
Of snakes
And types of
Fear
That overcomes
The desire
Of the gilded generation
With which industrial war was the solution
To everything.
Body count back home
Now they
Have the
Next surge
Pump and dump
And then they have to pick the next battleground
Of limited war

.BALDWIN@GMAIL.COM

To dump the over heated
Filth of commodity fetish
Production.
If we had a poetry based economy
Probably we would and a dumping ground for that
And mechanized
Tech
That turned
Every walking
Citizen

Into a soli
Of attention de
Screen held up to a w
Wh
They could pick the most interes
Aspects of the jungle la
But if Charlie is in th
Belt hugg
Cl

Overrunning
On the offensive
Knowing each LZ
And pulling tight
And far from Howitzers
Every thing out of the screen
Is interesting
Every dream of a jungle is a return to the
Struggle to overcome
'The other' in the primordial ooze
Of the jungle floor
From which you will return.

I do miss the equator.
The way it always grows
On everything
Eats it daily
And how the worst
Passivity
Places the middle brow
Over
Into

Worrying for the boys
Who will only be young men
That the old men will kill off.
They do worry for that
When they should worry for themselves
In cold cornfields.
Boys will be boys
In seven billion
You must spend their rare gold testosterone
Any time you see it.
And the tech

PHILLIP.BALDWIN@GMAIL.COM

Of the hand held phone
Is like the car that turns to a tank
It seems to make it easier
Then it becomes ubiquity
Like the jungle.
Then it becomes
The master prosthetic
Like the gun from the gunship
Like the car that 'makes it easy' to
Over come the city

That it over came.
Like
The love
You wish to say
To
The far off
Solider

Blasting through the walls of fallugia.
Like the regret
That you need these things
And attack
The people who don't need.

LIP.BALDWIN@GMAIL.COM

MIND-PUSH VERSE

PHILLIP BALDWIN

Who could believe the next pump and dump scheme?

The market is supposedly
Surging
At the same time
Millions couldn't hear
The music stopping

Who can?
Hear it.
Bad is what is
Ganged up on:
Ridiculed by
Enough shysters

All of this happens in a late spring
Smell of
Showers
Trees
And a fight against a
Winter near the heart
Distant places
Overage
Random selves return to selves
Others to other
Imperatives
Not seen as spheres
Of
Courage.

Courage is light
And applied like a
Cut and paste essay
You would be lucky if one of the
Petulant customers
Would apply
Themselves

Smoke filled rooms
Of
The same cast
Who would expect
They cannot expect the leaves to smell this
Green and deep
Though
The air is like a humid winter
Winter
Of
Barren emotion
From a petulant
Fetishized
Customer
Who thinks knowledge?
And the self transformed through the spheres
Is something consumed?
It is produced.

Who could believe the next pump and dump scheme?

Yet though I try to produce myself
In an ancient hand task it is
Seen as
That which is on the lot
And if it isn't it is defective.
Damaged by the
Vicissitudes
Of
Use
Fear and desire were the transports
Against a stream of
Other hungers.
Being is nothing
Not touched
Not smelled
Against the flowers of scant parks
Without time.
It is time
And what you wish to make of it
Out of a thoughtful desire
That gives you grasp.
Handholds
In the bargain with the devil
Meant to be guilt
That all you guide the vessel with
Is fear and desire?
Either side
Minimal
Taking from
Each change the extension of men
Make
On
The central nervous self
Central
To the smell of spring
And central
To be held
Against
The fear and desires of
That fickle gender...
I wish I could see myself produced
Over being which is only time...
And not consumed
By righteous others.

PHILLIP.BALDWIN@GMAIL.COM

As I would place my self
On a hill
And watch
All of the world
Come up to the edges.

.BALDWIN@GMAIL.COM

Human needs

Faustian Society Contemporary societies have at least four characteristics:

-- they use technology to overcome the limits of the world;
-- they use simulations and virtual realities as substitutes fo what they can't yet get from the world directly;
-- they hold to an ideology that says the acting out of fantas a form of art, entertainment and liberation;
-- they view physical reality; society and mind as forms of illusion or as something much like illusion.
This essay provides the broadest possible overview with wh to understand contemporary culture.-Sherry Turkle

They have the book writing
Essays
Written in skin
Lao Tzu
Out in the woods
Fights against
The technology of the air born castle: Confucius
Knowing is are primal mode
Living is primary
Thinking is secondary
Always embedded into a world
Thinking
As they all do
Being
Dasein
Specific to the coast huggers: custom
Embedding him in a life world.

Out in the wo
Technology first appears as a ch
And as a be

It cons

The woods has becomes
A life world of
Boxes in the hand
Girls needed
Connection
Boys needing a chance

Outside a world
Gnostic Arkons
Trap the body in rings
Looking out
In the woods it can become a prison too.
The motion of things

PHILLIP.BALDWIN@GMAIL.COM

Is ideal
In math
Opposed to living
Being doesn't come to being
Before becoming
Becoming comes
And sitting to make a choice
To find being is

False.
Objects don't flower
Becoming is
The boy's hand on the smart phone
Thinking there is a world to
Connect with a woman...
Arkons trap the spark of spirit in the body?
Is this the first prison?
No

There are techniques of transcendence
Always
Equate intellect with things
Smell deep the hyacinths
In a empty lot garden
Forge away

With false free time
Have tea with Lao Tzu
Look up at the sky
Dasein
Do not distract
From the body.

Faustian Society Contemporary societies have at least four characteristics:

-- They use technology to overcome the limits of the world;
-- They use simulations and virtual realities as substitutes for what they can't yet get from the world directly;
-- they hold to an ideology that says the acting out of fantasy is a form of art, entertainment and liberation;
-- they view physical reality; society and mind as forms of illusion or as something much like illusion.

LIP.BALDWIN@GMAIL.COM

Envy in the winter of time

Around,
Round,
Through,
Blockage,
They do not make,
Or produce
They criticize.
As if it is a Socratic art.
Specialized...
A culture in the beginning winter
Of all of the ideas it seeks to work
Out.
The arch
Can you see it from the hands?
The hands
Technis
A strategy from the eyes
Animal tactics
As if
The hands represent
Action...
The eyes theory.
This was the real was
To make
Tactics for survival.
The thought princes had thought
That
This was the best way
You could
Prevent the overcoming
Of humanity
By technics.
Most animals have it.
Seldom there is an animal
That encrusts the foam of its being
So that it overcomes the
Basic strategy of loving survival.
Technics
Is what the fat-assed 'critics'
Talk about as if drips and drabs
'Out there' are bits that they take
Of a meeting with those still passionate
To make. DIY.
Plants are dropped and blown on seeds
Helpless to a destiny...
Animals
Mostly
Binocular
Predators
See

PHILLIP.BALDWIN@GMAIL.COM

And after surviving
They deal
With the infinite directions of
Desire.
Vast,
Vastness
Which could be covered by love
After a meal
The will to being
But
There is that other
Technis.

Envy is the only passion
In the digi-democracy...sphere of
All that pass
Over the dyads of
Individual mother wombs.
Love is the central question
Of hand and eye
To move us back
From the technis for itself
Texting ourselves
Into hermit holes.
Envy
Is what Tocqueville
Saw emerge out
Of vast lands...glue...

Text your way out of technis
Junior.
Make
That person
Do what you want
Not. Or
Help you kill the stag
Not the tiny hare.
Envy is the last passion
In the winter decadence
Of a society.
Envy blankets the first winter chill
Apocalyptic thoughts inside
Each fallout shelter
Envy is the real motive
For the collection of guns
Envy moves to water and air
Envy supersedes life
Immersed in
The sex act
Envy

LIP.BALDWIN@GMAIL.COM

Makes one post from
Alexandrine hermit holes
Envy from Magian tunnels
That point downward
Toward Satan's
Dwell
Weighing the heart against the feather of
Good technis.

PHILLIP.BALDWIN@GMAIL.COM

MIND-PUSH VERSE

PHILLIP BALDWIN

MY NOT-SELF IN SLEEP

"We expect more from technology and less from each other."
— Sherry Turkle, Alone Together: Why We Expect More from Technology and Less from Each Other

If sleep is still a mystery of what to give to the self
What is texting?
'It is the inability to have true delicious solitude'...she said.
To know it is
Not
To rearrange the fragment
Of the gift self
Always
As a way
To make
Surface glue to the ot
The impulse
Make a
With the 'ot
But it fails in just t
I share small chunks of myself
As
They drift into the mouth
Of debt
Near debt
Never debt to sleep.
What is the world doing
When they cannot be
In the place there are at?
It is a small exercise to redress
The commodity self
Every click puts it 'out there' so that
It can seem to be
'Liked'
As it was shared.
What about that self
That isn't shared?
Raised as a pampered self
Where 'everybody is alright'
No they aren't
They are seven billion
Six and nine tenths of which are fodder
Of degrees.
'You are unique' means
That there are fragments of self you can share
Into the void
Of plenty.
I face sleep with screens
I wouldn't have or keep my job without

PHILLIP.BALDWIN@GMAIL.COM

E-mail…sending off daily splinters as
I send off bits of sleep to the mystery of utility.
Each constant phatic touch
Doesn't add up to
A brace of
Connection
As troubled sleep doesn't add up
To the restaging of the mind
And memory.

Solitude
Is what is needed.
To 'share' might just mean,
Like 'sleep' is the theater of memory-dreams
That I think my giant gift-culture
Is to shout
My fragile being
As an insect
To the history of seven billion
I am now entitled to 'share'
As I am to sleep…
But not.
If I cannot be with my self undistracted
I cannot be with
Any other
Others
Gliding across streets
But how do I make purpose of time
Where each zombie is somewhere else
The old still wish to train
All for pyramids

Making them
And only climbing them
To build?
Together together
Is
A score
A

Continuous tone
I try to sell my day labor
To pay
For my open time
Every 'virtue' thrust me there
Like a stream from sleep soon turned
To whitewater.
I will try
Try to meet
Try to see
My loved as
Some self in solitude…
Some way of not expecting much more from
Technology.
Some connection.
More
From the false.

THE SPHERE.

Sleep the dyad
Like
The mother
In womb
Knowing is only hearing
Collapsed into spheres
Of the megalopolis.

Then bubbles
Out of scant
Contacts
Yet I deal with dozens
Of young minds
Not curious
Of where they are at.

Mimetic
Then
Known
Enlightened
Not
Seeing
Foam

Is the way is flows
Then
Is a sketch
Then is a shaman
Manipulates nature
And where we are at
The foam of the city
Then the connected world
Reconstructing some
Other
At a distance
Afraid of solitude
Like intimacy.

They left.

MIND-PUSH VERSE

PHILLIP BALDWIN

THREE STATES

Appolonian, Magian, faustian:
I can touch, I can see, I
Can hope through mind.
Multiple worlds made

By
Deceivers and
By the self.

Self on the half self
Of hope above animals:
The Greeks made their
Syllogistic buildings
From the outside in.

The Magian moved
From some
Distant
Zoroaster
To
See

Projections before projections
On
A cave wall
Basilica bath,
Then the cathedral/
Mosque.
The Faustian
Hoped
That
There was no
Hell to pay
in projection.

There is no heaven but that
Of modern movement
From the logic on the inside...
Then the inside of the DNA
The code

That could become projection...
Could become
Anything.

Maya is illusion
But
Colliding Brahman
Talk
To Faustian
Maya is everything.

It first deceives
Like my hope of

PHILLIP.BALDWIN@GMAIL.COM

Return: of stuffing the individual
Harmonica
In the mouths of personal criminals
Then
Maya
Is our mere ability to see: it is all we have
Work
Ritual
Gridded orthoganals that move out of sfumato
Into ways we
Expect our intimates to move:
'I found, I said to that man at the garden party-yee of
The broken-heart-from-a-german-Phd.-model:
I found no algorithm
To them or their beauty...
Nor their rapacious appetite to
Envelope themselves in
Nests with projections, and you as
Pack animal...' so I said.
You are right...he said.
Maya in the last...after creation,
Projection, is dissection
Of the 'real'
Which was the interior
To the Faustian
Math on the inside
Is the strand of the DNA.

I hope their ferocious
Taste
For the best men,
Like the bride burned alive in
The limo of her bachelorette party, is that they find
The illusion of home
With
A man who might love them for a second,
Which might be all time.
Like cave paintings, wide-screen-TVs to
Place their time out of time.
She burned dead.

Off to the hope of transgression
Back to the chaste.
The Greeks loved to touch...the bounded...
The proportioned,
The shedding of Maya
Decomposed
By limiting space.
The cave
Project

-BALDWIN@GMAIL.COM

Burst with
Gothic plant spires
And Chartres
Windows of bursting glass
Against pagan ground Maze:

To touch the infinite
Is
A pleasure maze
Of loss.
Yet the modern
Calculating insect
Queen bee or drone

Is to do dirty to those
Proxemic next…
And then to atone
In severed Maya…

Smoke billows against an infinite spring sky
Cold air is like the hope of a pagan death
Where you could burn all intimates within your
Death ship
And sleep a hero's return
Medusa's head
Is that
You hold
Up
Final
To Maya's grace.

PHILLIP.BALDWIN@GMAIL.COM

Rock, paper, scissors, over day

In Leone
Bronson,
Fonda
Robards
Make for
An engine.
Move
Like some generative
Story
Upon
Flatness
Dark room
And men
Bros
Scanning
The landscape of their faces
To see what to do/and/or
What not to do.
To move without loitering
I think
Fonda was the rock,
Robards was the scissors
And
Bronson was the paper
Covering over
With a vengeance.

How I would like to stuff some
Mouths with harmonicas too.

This would make the
landscapes of their
Faces
Understand.
Know.
Place
Swim back in memes
As ocean liquid
Behind the rock
Stone
Crust
Of face.
Cut
The given mechanism
Money sucks
Scissors cuts
Paper enfolds
With
Memory
And
Revenge.

LIP.BALDWIN@GMAIL.COM

How this could be
With no Cardinale
Is anybodies guess
But these men could be on their
Own
I guess
Women like territory
But now we are all
Mantel drive eunuchs
Across
The dusty surface
Men and women
And hope
There isn't a harmonica
To stuff
The flight of regret
Out dying mouths.

PHILLIP.BALDWIN@GMAIL.COM

DEADLY NARCISSCISM

I had an attractive friend who ended up dead face down..
This was in his one bedroom apartment
In the young-hipster part of town.
When they found him three days later
He was cold, stiff, and starting to smell...
Every gift of the gods were given him
And he didn't spend it well.
On his answering machine they found many of my calls
'Come back to the world of the trying'
'Don't wrap yourself up in
Self-loving regret
Scaffolded by the conquest of women'
I would said
It was left on
The machine with
Many more of my calls
Back to the living.

We think he went out
With pain killers
Over dose.
For he said he was 'never suicidal'.
He didn't need to be
Narcissism kills.
Who he 'could have stayed with'...
You can stay with none of them
Women are not musical chairs
For the narcissistic soul

Nor is booze
Nor are 'pain killers'
For somatic
Pains of anchored backs
Left in
The earth like roots
And there you
Twist in the wind on the heath.

Sleep is always troublesome too
And they think the sugar in booze
Will not wake them up
To the terror of three.

I have an accomplished woman friend
With the same affliction
Deep rootless narcissism
That finds an aesthetic in booze.
Her parties are all the same: they start with dinner
Nice
With the same cast a characters,
Who barely tolerate each other?

LIP.BALDWIN@GMAIL.COM

Where the womanless men
Retire to another room
To get high off their assess
And she stocks the dining room with young, attractive
Chinese graduate students
And she is the queen bee dangling
The young eastern flesh in front of these
Stoned men.
She berates men for being less than her
And doses her rootless ego
In the growing liquid of booze
She turns, party style, her turret toward me,
And lobs in
Misaimed veiled insults
Like mortar
And then she weaves
And then she falls off her chair.
Party over.
Stoned men linger as the crippled court of Lear
Raging on the heath of
Madness
A former beauty
Now rotten with

Toxin
Yet mad like the redeemed Lea
Never seeing who was at faul
The me
Empty-handed walk
Or they wanted into the down town nigh
She has started painkillers toc

I think
Through my only hope of stags over hares
With some posse, what sort of scaffolding do I need?
Narcissism is a fuel like coal:
It works and burns but is dirty.

Pure egoless se
Like the western Buddha'
Looks nice on pape
But it doesn't wor
In the great global monster that devours the egos of the worlc
It is a gift to be bor

And a bigger gift to be born beautiful.
I had a dream last night that I was prepped for an interview
And I tried to make an account of what I really did in life
On the big interview
That would make me proud and 'sell myself'
To a future self.
The host was famous but faceless
And I couldn't think of a singular thing 'to sell'
A part of me that then
I could also feel didactic with

PHILLIP.BALDWIN@GMAIL.COM

Of
It was Jung who said that
The dual impulse of
Eros, and didacticism
Cancel each other out
In a bad smell.

Beauties with enough
Of the curious
To keep moving
So they would never grow
And their inner calculating ugliness
Would in volute
On the outside like a poisoned skin.
Yes.
I have had a few women like that…
Their problem is narcissism
Like a winged seed looking for soil to land
And nothing is ever good enough
Or bad enough for their rotten ego.
Dilettante art, no discourse,
They are too beautiful and talented to be where they are
The ultimate commodity like children…the splinted self.
'You are sexist to say that!'
No
I listen to say that…I watch not lumping
The average behavior over time
But see the confidence of the young taut body
Against the ugly fat bodies who resort to pedagogy
Like a nerdy boy resorts to a band
For their peacock feathers.

They are too beautiful
Like my accomplished boozed friends
To meet a surprising final payment on the captured
'void'
Of birth.
Perhaps they teach women this
Perhaps they know it with every hormone in their body.
It is useless to even the score with pedagogy
When their smart young bodies move
Like tanks across conquered plains cities.
In the first blush of sunny May Day
Then show every inch of their body and bosom
Commodity, dignity, and the roots of narcissism are
So close
Brethren.
The entitlement of beauty kills the host
The entitlement of brains rots the host
The entitlement of willful career is

P.BALDWIN@GMAIL.COM

Like a car
The entitlement of final narciss
Not curious
Ends your life qu

For it is May Day today
And a sunny May like a beautiful woman/plumaged male.
In the beautiful knowledge camp
When information doesn't want to be free
It wants to be learned.

It is too easy to criti
From here in the narcissists petting zo
The univer
Knowledge becomes like booze or painki
When it forgets quiet liste
Curiosity even: 'what was I born with so many gi
Wisdom itself in rootless narcissism
When young children peck at books thin
They are iPa

If I could replace the scheduled narcissism
Of young and old beau
Of nerds and jo
Of band boys, and sensitive yoga po
Of young ad
Who still get their Asses whipped
Their parents
After shitting entitlements
If I could replace
The wandering narcissism of
The ADD traveler of the world
Not knowing where he or she is
Or the smart beauty who will never really be
Shutting down the market call
Because she can never like her ego.
If I could replace commodity
Narciss
With curio
This would be
And

And 'interesting'...
Where the best part of childhood is brought

And there is no better place than this

PHILLIP.BALDWIN@GMAIL.COM

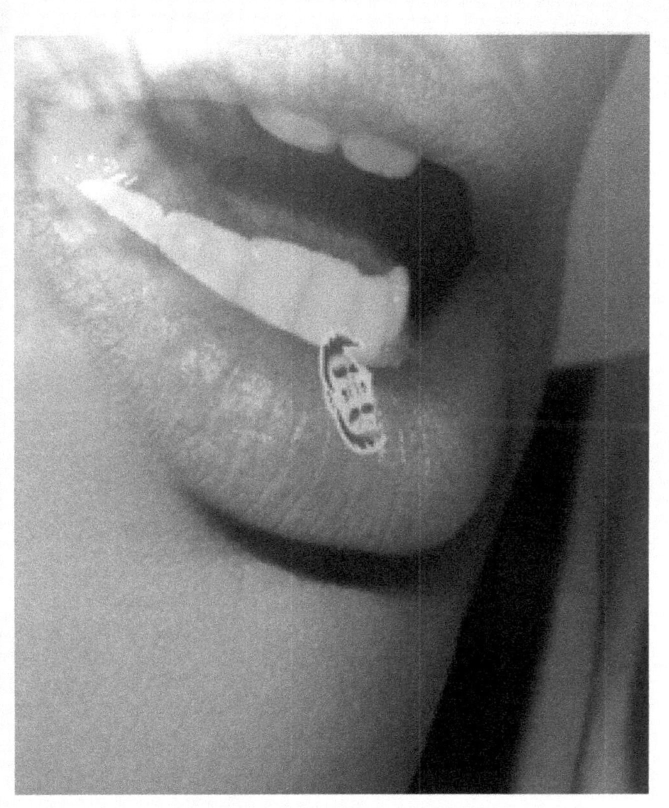

MIND-PUSH VERSE

PHILLIP BALDWIN

The lottery theory of
memes

I don't know
Where
I am
In
A bootstrap time
Of mine.
Past positive
Even
For the forks
Going
To worse than
Nowhere
Nobody...
Added
As
Layers
To present hedonism
Coffee
Smell in the morning
Cavendish
Dark, immersive tones
Memes
Remade.
Ideal perspective
Like Alberti
Laying down a net
That makes time a conic
Grid
Over hope
And the
Faux-attainable.

Who is a winner?
All paths
Of
Hard
Thought
Knows
The name?
No.
Running
In
Gridded parks
Are the same.

I learn from all forks in
the road
That double back

THE LOTTERY THEORY OF MEMES

PHILLIP.BALDWIN@GMAIL.COM

Somehow
Like the big chariot
learning
I do not wear the boat on
my head
As a sign of my
enlightenment
As I made it to the land of
the other shore
Near/nor choice of how I
changed
Myself
Once I got to the land of
the
Far shore idiots
Again.
I am a blight on their
landscape
Just as
On Sartre's foggy formal
garden
Visual disappointment
And vaporous
Solid 'other' appears
On given grid…
Showing up as the point
of void
Of nothingness
That looks back at me
too.

I wished to make
Past
A modeled behavior
Of that garden
Where I ran
In
Rome
All eyes
Conditioned by
Alberti's
Optimism
And all
Turned inward after uncle
Freud
Showed Bernes
How to
Lay down the desiring
Self
On a grid
Of want.

LIP.BALDWIN@GMAIL.COM

I cannot believe
Or want to
Think
That in the land of the far
shore
With no boat on my head
I move about people
Who think anything
unusual Unique
Childlike wonder even
Has to be
Placed
On a lottery grid
Of possible winners.
Alberti
Taken to
Extremes.
Taken to absurdity.
There
Is nothing
Off grid
And here
The sinister perspective
point
In the winner of dominant
memes
Like the run in Doria
Pamphili
Cues and codes
Of my explicit
dissatisfaction.
Can I live in my own
skin?
On the far shore?
Can I lay every particle?
Of a life negated
For that far shore
Only to
Land and say/know
I have not escaped
Myself?
Only to
Hold
Another
In a land of judgers
Who think they know your
perspective
As 'the' perspective
They acclimate toward.
I smelled the blossoms in
the spring
The cold rain
Made a big cold white
beautiful space

THE LOTTERY THEORY OF MEMES

PHILLIP.BALDWIN@GMAIL.COM

Cold
For a while
Hoping for the heat
Which it did.
And the entrancing
fecund bodies
Of foreign girls.

I had won the lottery.
You have to place
yourself on 'sense'
And then know
It is irregular
This logic of adjustment
Slavish
Approval
Never smelling cherry
blossoms,
Or Hyacinth (girls) in the
spring.
Wet heat rising from
ancient spring
Roads
And rides in motorinos.

I pity those on grids
Like lottery wins…
And those who stumble
into liquor store
Looking for their last
Far shore of broken/
shattered hope
In fragments to grasp
As it was another's fault
That they were placed on
the meme grid
In the first place.
Second.
Never knowing
Second
Time
Second
Other
On
Gridded greed for the girl
Fecund with her own
Hero's journey
Not mine
Sense?
It makes it
Not to wear the boat on
your head
Once your reach the far
shore

E LOTTERY THEORY OF
MES

P.BALDWIN@GMAIL.COM

Coldshore

Leaving?
We are all in exile
With our own half-
fragment use
Of Alberti's grid.
Approval?
It all is
On the authority of the
trip
Destination isn't as
important
As
Constant
Movement

And sighting 'the other'
on a foggy
Morning
On the outside.
Knowing
You are right with your
golden
Memes as if
You won
The lottery.

PHILLIP.BALDWIN@GMAIL.COM

MORNING WRITING ON THE BEACH:
THE WATER-MOON MOTELS OF JUPITER

Brave flowers push up
On my way to the beach.
Empty, sunny, slightly cold
This is the
Tenacious
Theater of seasons
Now with my now
Passing by old motels
Where I had my trysts
I salute.
Thee.
Anchors of intimate times in winter snow
And
Summer escapes to the moons of Jupiter
Where hot water
Glides beneath
Cool ice covering.
There the dunes of their best body
Many writing dunes
Covered with white sheets
And hotter burning
Furnace
Of seasons yet to come.
Even season less.
The warm always fights the cold
And
One day the sun will burst
First
Across the humid timeless equator
They say time speeds up with age…
It is the conveyor belt.
And lovers slow it down
So this/these are the most palpable
Anchors of the new
As we borrow from void
To give birth to self
Self is our debt
Where we collaborate
With Other
On journeys of inward drive
Making no hast
And stopping time
As markers and
Immersion
Even on these motel beaches.

LIP.BALDWIN@GMAIL.COM

What is wrong with the next have of souls?
Humanity?
I don't like to whine like a dinosaur
But they do never
Immerse
But scatter
As they with older lovers
Hold the unique grasp as timeless.
It was there
In these beach motels
I practiced long Tantra
With a colleague of the planet slow
And as we plunged into beyond the ice core
We melted in locked time
In the full emersion of the spine to mind
To contact
Creation.

What of these new walkers on the ice moon's crust
They never produce their immersion
But they make their vectors
They consume the experienc
Out of the chance of captivity
They are hoarse on those feeble who do not conform to
Implicit laws
And link every inch of their life with vector Smartphone
Pathetic.
They will never know Jupiter's moon's hidden hot core
For point
Perhaps lovers too
Are commodity stations?
They consume a priori.
The monastery of leaning is now a spa
They move quickly like insects
And I pity their bald experiences
How could they rip their carapace?
From their mantle…logic is the line of consuming
And credit
And think like media Nuevo Riche….

Herding instinct still in place.
It is the logic of the web…the lines
To avoid the infirm…
Children are like fascists
With brighter smiles

Outsiders are still punished.
For not knowing the implicit being.

PHILLIP.BALDWIN@GMAIL.COM

What logic they grasp is like a mantle
Of quid pro quo
Near mimicking mathematics
But not.

There is No imperative to 'be in time'
With something unusual…unique…produced.
This is a world without wonder
Like the anchors of lost motels
They seem to immerse into
The swarm of the herd
And diffuse outward
While inward
To loneliness.

The cure? To? What now? Vector worlds more
Salient than sitting
Rapt?

They produce their connections,
They purchase their experience.
Pre formed
Practiced.

As GPA turns to Credit number
The transition is simple.
Games of great 'stag and hare' dissolve
To small bewildered posses
Or lynching mobs.

That is them…I pity.
This is me…finding the past immersive anchors…even on this beach
As my kin crawled
On the shores
Of past coastlines
Where the interior was dangerous with huge animals
Take pleasure from immersing in the set,
Commoditized experience.

And the sea was
A repayment to the void.
I, perhaps, as my polychromic being
Crawled even on the shores on the wet moon of Jupiter
Beneath an azure ice sky
Like a green house hot
With hope
And there is/was
Staring into deep
Asian eyes
Less again…two on
Far planet shores.

This is me
Why should I make
My business of them?

They cannot be focused…always polychromic.
Poly-Chronos…as I hope my many times
Become anchors like motels
Rich ritual
Of saluting
For bliss surely in the mind of childless women
Where the goal is accident that never happened
But it is
Confrontation to produce/create is something unpleasant.

Abstraction in narrative is something avoided.
'Logic' in cliché produced 'experience' narrative is the norm…
To repeat marching orders.
To repeat the arrival of packaged time
Gives them the 'like'
Of knowing each MacDonald's is the same
Ten thousand miles apart.
This is not 'Americanism
As America is very much akin to
The wet Jupiter moon…
They know this
That when immersed they can be
As deep into the new that they never knew
Far Vikings
Far return
As you must come down a mountain
They never go up…not for the fear.

Creative finding vectors.
They
As mine is arrivals
Departures are an art
They say
The last one.
I say arrivals
That you then must leave
Like mountain tops
Thin air
Touch the top of an ice ceiling
Pay back the interest
And principle on
The loan of void
Perhaps threaten one life
Mine
A ladybug mounts my beach screen now…

PHILLIP.BALDWIN@GMAIL.COM

Still now...
But
In the losing in two
I shall make an art of arrival
Even as departure holds
For most
These tiny world-phones have shattered them
Into
Trillions of synapses
Never now glued again.

I need apt partners for trips to water moons...
Always.
And I don't always choose them wisely
For they can sink the vessel there...
Those
Once arrived
Unpacked
They will never forget
Beach motels
Like me
And return
As on a default of my loan from the void.

water-moon hotels of jupiter:
NING WRITING ON THE
CH

P.BALDWIN@GMAIL.COM

MIND-PUSH VERSE

PHILLIP BALDWIN

TIN CAN TRRAVEL

Tin cans contain
Lives
Flipped on highways
And long trains
Asking 'why'?
Move when all we need are bits?

We need the face time…credibility.
We need to make the mystery of birth and
existence
The principle by which we pay for the debt
Of punching a hole in nothing.

It is strange that the gift of something
Is paid back to other men
Women
And mostly children.
When the true 'capital' is
Void.

So it is struggle in tin can
Movement
To repay the debt of
Forming opinions
Snarks
Cynicisms
Bitching.

When we could
Have had
Nothing
And that is the return.
For void was the original bliss
Or the moment right after void

Where
It was a womb
And not a can
Moving, compact
And mother-drunk
We where complete in that
After void
Of full.

She was borrowed too
Pinioned by pappy
She couldn't help her power
To make something out

LIP.BALDWIN@GMAIL.COM

Of the bliss of
Void
She became all mass
And a liquid love for you and her
Now matched by tin cans.
Cars, trains, busses...beasts

Best
For travel...
And we ask why not? Why not did they
not?
Did they not
Have the desire
To meet in flatness
Online?

It takes too too much
To get anybody to care about the free'
Like free void
You must make it the dearest thing on earth
Precious meeting time to practice...
rehearse.
And not make the void so strange that
It becomes a relic

That takes price from an auction of
fetishists
You borrow against the void...in hopes of
return
And the price is so dear you think
Mass is slavery
It isn't...
And as mass was a gift
So mostly is void....
Don't borrow too much beyond
Given credit.

PHILLIP.BALDWIN@GMAIL.COM

I start with the mystery of morning's wake
For it's contrary was the
Evening's dissatisfaction
Should have moved
In a finite bundle of weekends
Through the city of doors
Where the herding animal
Moves
In isolated groups isolated.
Contrary to the bright Sunday morning
Is the infinite night city
Both could go nowhere.
The implication of the bright morning waking
Is neither walk in night or wake in day
From Saturday to Sunday...
But the sleep that is also far
Infinite
As that.

Kali sits on her dead Shiva
As it isn't death within the history of woman
But a type of death
Of ADD within city, sleep, Sunday wake.
'Tell me what I want'
Is the cry of those at night
And
Let me find a quite sun place
Is that of the readers of the morn.
Perhaps the contradiction
Of night's dark walking dissatisfaction
And of an infinite embrace of morning sun
Is the contradiction in copulation...
The fourth term

That generates the rest.
For this there is image....
Even image to the touch
Or compulsion
Or a type of materialism
Born in authority
And
If lucky
Tempered in desire.

Meaning lies in the difference between concepts
As brazen as existing
And ceasing to be...
All the modern submarine documentaries
On how the absurd building of form
Spends our tax money
And squeezes a type of slow suffocation
From those who are taught that those three things are theirs:
wake, walk, and sleep...
War machines are the opposite of sex...then of love.
They spend without the particle public
Having a say

CE CLAY
LIP.BALDWIN@GMAIL.COM

That this form of invisible war
Is obsolete...
That other 'dissenters' ...haven't a right
To shadow our shallow society
Unless they know they are
Consciously.
Wake, walk, sleep, sex...

Semiotic
Block on
The rest of a year...
Build
But build
As
A known
Block
To
Movement
Always
To work off bad food
Again.
Walk to
Move
And find the door of the night
Dissatisfied
Grandiose
And replicate
Unconsciously
Like reptiles

Stream
A stream across
Eyes
That find
That they need faster eyes

To live completely
Sleep
In trouble
And sex
Not out of humanity
But in materiality
It is impossible to touch
The others with the phone
As now it is impossible
To touch with copulating skin
Or penetrating eyes.

PHILLIP.BALDWIN@GMAIL.COM

Theory of loitering: cheesy cake

I pull four times from my
Shell: recalled is time…memory through felt sleeplessness.
I sit on immediate time through
Presence and feeling the internal call
I call on subjective time
Of the ant-clock, chronos measured
Polychromic scorned but
Always used
Half as bad
And staying
In a coma

Of
Feel.
I have my seasonal time
Kairos
Discerned
Snow
Cold
Inside
Warm
Where I can
Get the most done
Before the humid heat.

I remember
In the edge jungles
Of suburban Singapore
To cross a hundred yards in the morning heat
Was like dragging
Lead weights
On legs
Arms

That swung
In humid air
Though I loved the birds
And the flowers
That bloomed every morning
And the animals
That ate everything leather
Which was dead shell to them.

I am
Still
In that realm with the herds
Of unconscious incompetence
Of the existence of relevance
No they are…
For me
Like Socrates
I am in the realm of conscious incompetence.
Know

P.BALDWIN@GMAIL.COM

That I don't know
Knowing that even that humid first
Yard
Was a trip like all others?
First step
...It wasn't difficult from sleep
Or
Out
It was difficult because there were no seasons
Every day was July.
The sun sank like a lead ball
Every pattern of desire
Became frustration
Of types
Of heat
Of jungle eating
But the smallest creatures.
I pity those
Who have never known this.... those who bitch about
The heat of July
With the cool of April
Late.
You cannot stay on the top of a mount
As you can't stay in a threshold of a d
Loiter
Talking to the gatekeeper beh
And the ravishing beauty within

Somewhere the unconscious competence
Makes you move and think
Of the flow which is not yours...
Never timed
Plychronic
Never because
It is like a summer reading of samurai
Who always come at you one at a time
Through the infinite division of time...
Knowing
That you fear
Simultaneity.
You don't.
For even the best movies
Are single pictures
Made to come alive throu
Speed and loiter
Given up to your caring of li
All li

CHEEZY CAKE/THEORY OF LOITERING.

PHILLIP.BALDWIN@GMAIL.COM

Map of the Simulacrum

Spengler: Egypt was a time before time…
The reason they lasted long in their time
Before our time
Was that they denied death.
Vast was the terrain of death,
Decay.

They built a map of that land
With fingered religion
Paper flatness like their papyrus
Linen
And everything that can be flat, folded
And covered with dry dust.

Then they walked across their map
As if it were real: they took out the dead organs
Of pharaohs
And they put this
In alabaster jars…
They embalmed them in paper
Cloth

Linen
For the 'afterlife'
The simulacrum of a future hope,
And then they moved
The big hope
Against hope

That became another real:
Vast pyramids
For workers thought to like
Their task in the sun
And drinking beer
At night.

Against the edges of desert.
Then they
Moved across the map of the map
In ritual, barges packed with 'permanent' things…
How they are
Yes

Permanent
In dry desert tombs
Against the thieves
Who believe
In only the second layer: the map to steal
Within.
Their barges
Stuff
Wooden toys
Models
Mummified crocodiles

LIP.BALDWIN@GMAIL.COM

Had nothing to do with the first time
Of labor, shoes, and practical gold
Yet

It became the most 'real'
Against death
And therefore
The biggest future hope
To administrate.
Plow

Irrigate.
The four realities
From the real labored touch
Of the lover
To the life on the map of the lover
With the reptilian
Vectors
Have skewed emotion
Envelops the hope of the last life on
It.
Simulacrum.... the unreal of the real.
So it is to return to touch....
The labor of love after the labor
On the map
For vast stone things

For the hope after the death
And the reality of sex
For the worker
In the pits
At the base of the
Stone.
Sphinx...

Knowing
That the riddle is
You can believe any of the four
Realities
Stone, map, fantasy afterlife,
And the labor for the fantasy real
But it is best to go up and down them
Without regret
And you can make it through
Them.
Up and down.
Sideways.
Always
As they administrate
What is yours from the beginning.

PHILLIP.BALDWIN@GMAIL.COM

BOTH ENDS OF THE KNIFE ARE THE SAME

In the world the value of either end of the knife is the same, but hold the blade and find out the wrong way of living. - Rene Duamal

Twisting up the public
So that it becomes
The exposed secret agenda
Of
A small group of
Disappeared people.
Twisting up
Holding raw
The end of the blade of expectation...
'How to live' as floating memes
About friends, family and lovers,
Where sex had more to do
With the ecstatic
Pleasures
Of falling on
Authority.
Twisting up
Throwing myself against numbers
Where
I coral
Herd the young like cats
Against borderless fences
In territories not too far...
I consider deep pleasure of
Questions and curiosity
Hold
Forth
Move
Group
Job is an interesting case of a knife
Used by the devil and by a God...
'I bet he wont turn on you
If you use him to the core
Beat him like a dog
'The bet is on'
Said the god
Who remembered how he threw the devil
Out of heaven
For being similar so slavish in admiration
Of 'him'...he couldn't stand
The reflection
Of a world too full of handles
And no blades...

TH ENDS OF THE
IFE ARE THE SAME
LIP.BALDWIN@GMAIL.COM

You are on.
And so
He took a trusted knife in Job
And battered it
To every point where the
Abused…like Abraham, like even Christ
Who is really in all men
Not in a piss poor deity…
Of tribal herding men…
Use him up
Said Satan…the genius
So he finally says there is no
Big god
And I always knew evil to be
Only ego's imperfect sight
There is no radiance
To sentient loss
And when he begs to his friends
And family
And lovers…'no, I am good…'
They say…'no, you really must have been bad…'
At the moment when Satan smiles to almost the edge of
The bet
Job covers himself with ash
At the Big Guy's revelation
And crusty little desert people
Needed an alpha dog
That would stay in their dry hearts
Out of Egyp
No…I cover ash to represen
My sentience
Still has faith
That there is a good that has turned bac
To tes
Gate keep
When, I should say
I am the first and last authority
To awake
Buddha-style
To the material world
Of nothing
Where
Armies of students line up for abuse
Like happy sheep
And take debt that is a motivation
To belief
In the commodity fact that they are transformed
No
Said Job
I could have gotten my education
In ubiquity
In the pleasures of

PHILLIP.BALDWIN@GMAIL.COM

Capillary life…I could
Never have indebted myself to loss
To the end
Near end
Puss and ash
At the end
On a hard desert floor
Just to trust the Buddha within
I do now…I don't denounce you
Alpha dog in the sky and beta dog in
The crater
I could have soaked up my tragic
Beaten, pustuler soul
In curiosity as a balm
I am free in the biggest prison of the body.
I am free to know, to take
Ubiquity
Upon a mystery
Of why I am here getting bet upon
And why the 'best' and the greatest 'evil' bet on my good
Honest soul
And my curiosity that my fornicating parents made me
One hot night…. for that delicious curiosity
Not the stupid father in the sky
I have survived…in the wonder
Which is my capillary path
Back to this wonder
While all my former friends
Wonder why I lost it all…
You one percent will never wonder
About the energy simply bursting
From my contingent spirit
You will wonder how you could tap that
Ambiguity: is it slavish or is this
The aquiescence to all things
Things
All things there
All things material.
And from this point the two big fools
In the pit and height
Can evaporate
Into my wonder
And my foolish small thoughts of authority
And there I am happy
About my path
And see Job's imprint on all
The real
The universe
And the delicious
Indifference
Of
Dirt.

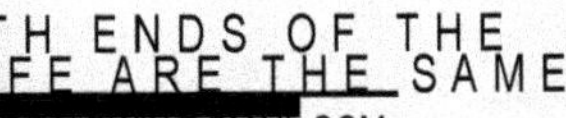

P.BALDWIN@GMAIL.COM

LUDENS/FABER: SATAN'S CONE

"A knife is neither true nor false, but anyone impaled on its bla
is in error."
— René Daumal, *Mount Analogue*

A play within...
As the sun raises so does the spring day
Teach of winter
So does the winter teach
Of forked roads
Pinioned
Upon
Flesh
So

Does it not remove
Any regret
As play of time.
I should play with time.
I should happen to play with the time
As it is work to think
Of an angle cast to earth by the greatest
Deity
For

Being too devote
And then, it is said
That when he was cast there
He hit the crust of the earth
And it slip like a silent meteor
Acts of god.
And there...in his bewilderment
Lucifer

Formed as slavish revil
And more than a cra
Of crust and golden stc
Cauterized the skin surf
Of spring d
Th
Cast dc
Was a co
Where at the bottom he
Burnt
Reject

SATAN'S CONE/LUDENS/
FABER

PHILLIP.BALDWIN@GMAIL.COM

And on the skin surface of a possible spring
There are beings that nag
And fight
And sometimes love.
Play is turned to work so that
Their young
Know nothing but work
That is now play.
Polyseme
Cold interpretation....
As seen never metaphor
To attend
In case
And in fact
And in a warm summer ay before smell.
And they came to the edge of Satan's crater
Ditch
And cone own to the molten core
And thought, then said to each other:
His was no play...he loved
The lord god as more than he.
...Perhaps he was punished for no more
Than this
But this is up to interpretation.
Then this is what attends obsession?
Short-term memory in holding?
This attends the perfect Boy Scout
A crater ditch cone
To live at frozen lake center
Where perhaps
When those of us surface crawlers are lost
We find the opening far and wide
And then think this must be
And we must avoid.
But there

For even the banal movement
Across the flatland commands
That we think of a pit
In ourselves so deep and cold
It makes our special spring day
Unobserved.
This is not good.
We can look over the edge of the crater
And there we will thin...only after knowing that he
Lives down there.... that we have it better
Crawling through a bland purgatory.
We half-do
Half-don't.
We surround ourselves with loves
And then cast them further down...
We compulsively obsess
On a bright day

LIP.BALDWIN@GMAIL.COM

And then
Forget this is precious borrowed time.
We dance at the edge of Satan's crater
And think we could scare and fool
Our friends
And one night
We walk over a beautiful spring meadow
Smelling the first hyacinths
There in late April
And then fall
Out of no good but negligence
Into another regretful
Rapture.

PHILLIP.BALDWIN@GMAIL.COM

SIMPLE PLOTS/an insect life

Questions, no answers.
All discourse is like a paddle
In a three inches deep river.
5000 miles wide.
Why isn't it called an ocean?
Because it seems to flow one direction
Into an apocalypse that is the making
Of obedience
Of flight
Of proximity
Of direction
Of flocking
And of complaining.

Questions for answers
How will the beauty of knowledge
Now put into its own bubble scheme
Fail?
Fall
Explode?
It will
Be pricked every time by Google
A search
'Here is the answer!'
So stop this blather.
This isn't' the epoch for the curious peasant.
But watch the peasant who
Takes wonder as a trip
A movement
An experience of limits

They have to know what the insect life is like
It is flocking where they should be learning
It is the shallows
It is the idea that they can buy it for the indebted price
And never think that they are producing the self.
They wish to be professionals who think
Though they are janitors of the machine

What is the insect life?
Toil but the pleasure of
The connected.
To know that others toil
It is hooking up on the weekend
And thinking you have arrived at a fragile sanctuary
It is thinking that your parents intimate life never matter
When it is the first thing on your mind.
What experience in the three-inch river

LIP.BALDWIN@GMAIL.COM

As wide as the world?
What is it that matters?
Insect life?
Even in the magic of the collective space
They want punitive results
They want punitive clicking
They want the pay to play
And moving,
Slogging
Over the sandy beaches.
To fast machine gun fire.
Encountering all who attempt the beach of intimacy
All who

Have the curiosity
Who wish to fall over the side
Of the canoe
Flowing in the 5k river
And hoping for to be drowned
In fathomless
Expanse
Of liquid
Knowledge

PHILLIP.BALDWIN@GMAIL.COM

MIND-PUSH VERSE

PHILLIP BALDWIN

www.ingramcontent.com/pod-product-compliance
Ingram Content Group UK Ltd.
Pitfield, Milton Keynes, MK11 3LW, UK
UKHW021050270726
13967UKWH00012B/143

9 781304 259103